The Book of Love

The Book of Love.

Published by the Facebook Analog Research Laboratory.

Designed by Jez Burrows. Set in Harriet by Okay Type.

Printed in Canada by Hemlock Printers Ltd.

ISBN: 978-0-9965642-0-5

First edition.

The BOOK *of* LOVE

Table of contents

Introduction

Suddenly, as a company, we were all talking about love, and the shipping thereof. What began as a single slide in an All Hands soon became a ubiquitious internal conversation, which at its best was a call for a renewed sense of empathy, but at its worst became a non-sequitur hashtag.

We set up an email address and a voicemail service, and asked Facebook employees to tell us about love. We asked the same of a handful of writers and artists outside the company, too. We wanted to widen and explore the interpretation of love, and this book is a record of what we found: stories about tragedy, memory, marriage, childhood, hope, heartbreak, and—perhaps most importantly—the often uncanny intersections of love and technology.

To make a book about love, first you have to know it will always be unfinished. We didn't intend to make something comprehensive or definitive (that book would be much heavier), just a collection of work from both inside and outside our walls that might hopefully illuminate the corners of love we forgot, overlooked, or didn't even know existed.

The Facebook Analog Research Laboratory
July 2015

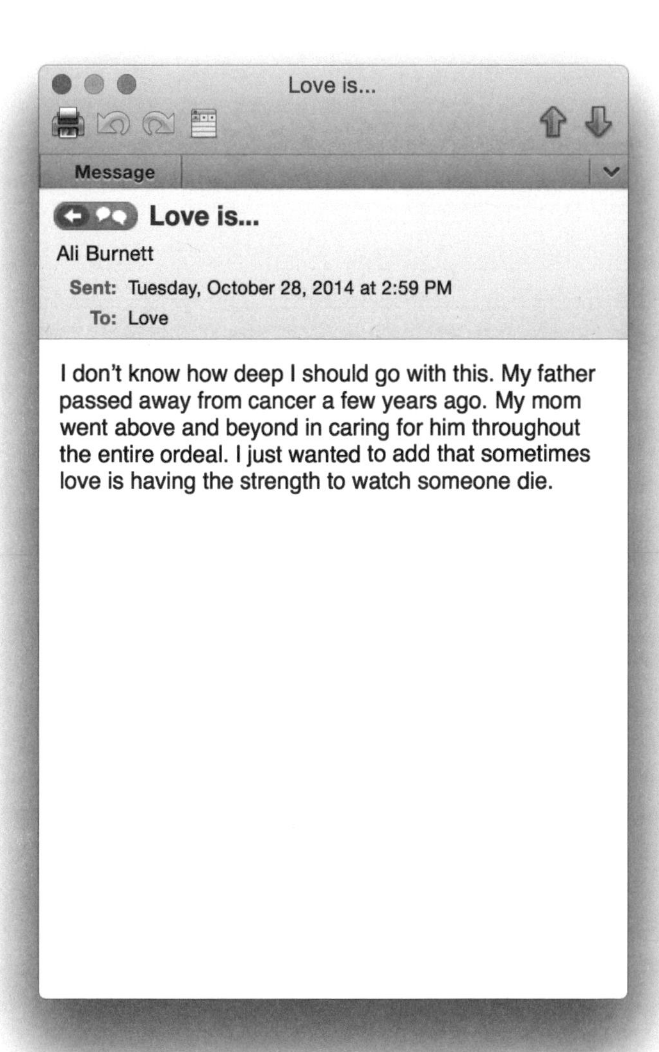
Love is...
Message
Love is...
Ali Burnett
Sent: Tuesday, October 28, 2014 at 2:59 PM
To: Love
I don't know how deep I should go with this. My father passed away from cancer a few years ago. My mom went above and beyond in caring for him throughout the entire ordeal. I just wanted to add that sometimes love is having the strength to watch someone die.

Something To Remember

Sean Michaels

The problem for Theo was not that he still loved Jeanie. It was that he still remembered what loving Jeanie was like. He remembered exactly what it was like. He went about his days without any longing in his heart; without any ache or ask, without any unasked question to his ex-girlfriend across the city, no wondering about her heart or if she might text him or if he should text her, something like *XO* or *XXO* or *XooO*, just two to four characters. No none of these things were resting on his spirit as he called suppliers or tallied inventory—they were two years finished, 65 miles apart, on good but not great terms, and he knew he no longer loved her, not now that she ran Color Runs and kept a blog about rosé.

But sometimes Theo would be stooped over a crate of clementines, a crate containing smaller crates of clementines, and he would remember precisely what it felt like to be in love with Jeanie Cortland Martinez, in love and gazing at clementines, a bowl of clementines, three clementines he had picked for her and placed in a little bowl, and Theo would be undone. Marty would come in the back, by the loading dock, and Theo would be stooped over a pallet of diminutive California oranges with his hands on his thighs just bawling.

"You OK?" Marty would ask.

"Ahhhhhhh," Theo would reply, drawing a breath like a man who has been holding his breath underwater.

So strange to remember a feeling that you do not want to

be able to remember. Like a book on a shelf: *Oh, there it is, that love I had for Jeanie Cortland Martinez.* Only you want to take the book and throw it in the fire. You want it not to be on that shelf, blue and silver, beautifully bound. Theo wanted to think of Jeanie and only think of Jean, Jean Martinez, not Jeanie. He wanted to forget what it was like to say the word *Jeanie*, the name *Jeanie*, with tenderness. But he could remember. He could still remember: he would try it, muttering the name under his breath, and it would be just right and just the same and suddenly it was like all of Theo's easy, happy, settled life was a barren land of shit.

He decided it was like a kind of muscle memory. He was typing a review of *The Wire* Season 2 box set into Amazon when he decided this. Like how his fingers just danced across the keyboard, knew where and what to type: his old love was like that. Automatic patterns, neural pathways that hadn't yet been rewritten. So Theo set out to rewrite them. Anything it was easy to remember—the way they'd sit on the couch with their feet touching, the way he'd dance with her, the way he'd murmur Jeanie's name—he tried to reprogram. While he watched *The Wire* Season 3 he laid the soles of his feet on the glossy back of his dog. At cousin Nora's wedding Theo danced Jeanie's favorite disco moves with Aunt Sue. He murmured the brand names of cereals in intimate tones of voice. *Shredded Wheat*, he whispered, and he also appended texts to employees with tags like *XooO*. Not new, young employees, but old-timers, workers who had been around a while. *Luv u too*, they'd text back. Sometimes Theo would see a message like this and begin to cry.

How could it still feel so near? Two years already but Theo saw something like *Luv u too* and instantly it was as if he was back on that work trip to Miami in 2009, his phone pinging in his pocket, a message from Jeanie just before noon.

"Do I miss her?" he asked himself seriously one night. "No," he said. "No. No, I don't! I just remember her."

Did he want to forget her? Theo didn't know. If he had the choice to forget her, like in that movie *Eternal Sunshine*, would he take it? Theo remembered when they watched *Eternal Sunshine* together, how Jeanie's eyes had welled up and how later that night they made love so tenderly, so deliberately, as if they wanted to memorize each breath and touch, as if they wanted to count them almost; nine, ten, eleven.

Theo was at the store, showing a new stockboy where the bulk stuff went and the refrigerated stuff went, and the little locked cage for the alcohol, when a message came out over the P.A. "Theo, phone for you." He left the kid in the cheese pit and went over to the phone by the staff bathroom, the grotty brown one with the tangled cord.

"Hello?" he said into the receiver.

"Hello?"

"Yeah, hello? Who is this?"

"Is that Theo?"

"Yeah, who is this?"

"It's Jean," she said.

"Of course," he said to Jeanie. "Hey! How's it going!"

But what Theo was really thinking was *I didn't remember her voice I didn't remember her voice I didn't, remember, her voice*. And when the call was complete, and Theo had agreed that his store would sponsor Jeanie's community library barbecue, he sat down on an upside-down container that had once contained mayonnaise. He held his face in his hands. He didn't know if he was sad or happy but actually he knew he was very sad; he was sad at life, adult life, which feels like a series of desolations, one thing after another getting razed or taken away. Even the memory of his love for Jeanie, he'd lose that too. It was equivalent to an old email address, a bad TV show, the name of his third grade teacher. And Theo decided that all he wanted out of living was that not everything feel equivalent: that just one, or two, or twenty things sit apart.

He went back to the cheese pit.

LOVE IS A MANY SPLENDORED THING

Ode to the wall outlet

Melissa Gregoli

Let me use you only for a moment—
push into you, against you
rely on you to

fill me up.
Revive me
like the revolutions of Venezuela.

Inspire me as lightning
demands the leaves of grass
to stand taller.

Electrify me if you must
to remind me that life still
stings in my veins.

Please—
don't turn off.
I wait for your response
under the covers,

I wait for your open mouth
to give me what I need—
your attention,
your power.

LOOKI
LOVE
GREAT
OF LI

G FOR
N THE
FOREST
E

Why—when it comes to children—love may not be enough

Alain de Botton

Anyone of childbearing age will be surrounded by examples of catastrophic parenting in their own and previous generations. We hear no end of gruesome stories about breakdowns and resentments, shame and addiction, chronic failures of self-confidence and inabilities to form satisfying relationships. And at the root of all these varieties of suffering, one central cause sticks out: a lack of love. It was because the parents were remote and domineering, unreliable and frightening that life has never been quite complete.

From such failures, a major assumption has come to dominate modern ideals of parenting: that one must, above all else, love one's child thoroughly, with immense sympathy, gentleness and kindness and that if one does so, the child will develop into a happy, loving and fulfilled human being.

This is the Romantic view of parenting and it is at its most vivid and self-assured in the early years, especially at moments when the child (finally) lies asleep in its cot, defenceless before the world.

Yet, despite immense investments and profound devotion, one is—gradually—liable to be inducted into a far more complex and challenging set of truths: that love is not a universal panacea and that giving unconditional affection is no guarantee of all the results one had hoped for.

The terrifying 3am truths about parenting run a little like this:

1. You are a punchbag

The blades of your child's remote-controlled helicopter snapped after five minutes, just as you were starting to get the hang of flying it. The fault lies squarely with the manufacturers. But, sadly, they were not present in the kitchen—so, at once and not for the first time, you became the target for the raging disappointment of your child.

The repeated bad behaviour is surprising of course (it wasn't meant to be that way), but it is a perverse sort of tribute to you nevertheless. One has to feel rather safe around someone in order to be this difficult. You certainly weren't so tricky with your parents when you were young, but then again, you never felt so loved. All those assurances—'I will always be on your side'—have paid off perfectly: they have encouraged your child to direct their every frustration and disappointment onto the loving adult who has signalled that they can, and will, take it.

2. You have to be the spoil sport

Human nature has a strong—and exceedingly inconvenient—bias towards indulging in whatever is most immediately pleasant and fun. And yet the central, unavoidable task of being a loving parent is to encourage the child to delay gratification in the interests of longer-term fulfilment. That's why there will be fights. Constantly.

After all, it is so much nicer to play Minecraft than to learn how to spell 'scythe' or 'embarrassment'; so much more amusing to see what happens if you put a hosepipe in the car's exhaust than to do maths homework; so much better to read a magazine than brush one's teeth, so much more gratifying to stay in bed than have a shower.

Out of love, a parent must—all the time, in small ways and large—say no. And for this, they will be severely punished. They will be treated as if they had arbitrarily made up the mechanics of tooth decay or had designed an economic system where the playing of computer games was disconnected from a capacity to pay bills. They will be punished for always bringing up unwelcome facts. And they will be very unfavourably compared with people who give the child whatever they want—because they just don't care about them. It's the thoughtless hedonistic characters, the ones who suggest all-night cartoon sessions and come around with iPads, who will be viewed as the heroes while the caring, denying parent has to contend with being called a 'meanie' and, later perhaps, a fascist.

3. You have to exert authority rather than teach

The dream is to coax the child into doing certain difficult things without ever having to demand they do so by force. The dream is not to have to 'exert authority', by which one means, bypass reason in order to impose a conclusion. The dream is to teach, and never to rely on the more basic weapons, like the assertion that one is the older, richer, bigger party.

One thinks with distaste of the Victorian parent demanding obedience simply by saying 'I am your mother, I am your father'. To the child, the meaning of these words, mother and father, have changed entirely; they now mean merely 'someone who will make it nice for me' and 'someone I will agree with if I see the point of what they're saying.'

But attempts to teach and appeal to a child's reason can only go so far. Whatever one says in a gentle voice, the children won't eat vegetables; they won't want to get out of bed in the morning; they will want to mock their younger brother or sister; they won't stop playing the computer game.

When the child is very small, it is easy enough to deal with these protests: one can just lift them up or distract them in some kindly way for a moment. But later, by six, one has to use authority: one must simply assert that one knows best without explaining one's reasons.

The child wouldn't have the relevant bits of experience that would render one's lessons comprehensible. A nine-year-old girl cannot understand how humiliating her six-year-old brother physically is a bad idea because this might make it hard for him to relate easily to women when he is older. It isn't her fault she can't understand. It would indeed be wholly unreasonable to expect a nine-year-old to be reasonable—and correctly comprehend the force and direction of adult concern.

The dream is that one will be able to pass on insights to the child that were painfully accumulated through experience, and thereby save them time. But in the absence of experience, insight doesn't work. One cannot rush children to conclusions; one cannot spare them time. They will need, with difficulty, to make many of the same mistakes (and a few new ones too) and waste a good part of their lives finding out what you already know full well.

4. You can't make things too nice for them

Modern culture is deeply vexed—and appalled—by the thought that development might require suffering. We have been traumatised by the barbaric old-fashioned enthusiasm for punishment, the view—expressed by generations of sadistic Victorian school masters—that success demands pain, that there is a necessary relationship between early discomfort and humiliation and later strength and 'character'.

But we have not just rejected the Victorian mechanisms

for inflicting suffering (the cold showers, the beatings), we have for the most part sought to abolish suffering altogether. Kindness has been triumphant.

And yet this attempt to abolish suffering involves waging a counter-productive and ultimately cruel war with the facts of human nature. We know from our own experience that we have at key moments grown through things that had a painful side to them: that there were terrors, rejections and disappointments that—in the end—made us more mature and better able to pursue our goals. We know that the drive to accomplish certain things, to master some difficult material, to win out over others, gained some of its power from fear and desperate insecurity. Because someone (perhaps a parent) didn't believe in us, we redoubled one's efforts. Because we were afraid of the consequences of failure, because succeeding was the only way to impress someone we loved but who wasn't easily impressed, we put on an extra spurt.

We desperately want our child to grow mature but without going through awful things. We hate being an agent of fear. We want always to cheer and to hug. We want everything to be nice. Yet we also know, in our hearts, that this can only be a path to ruin.

5. You can't guarantee their goodness

The Romantic view of existence sees all humans as fundamentally good from birth: it is only upbringing and a lack of love that corrupts and damages us and in the process, makes us cruel. Romanticism states that if only a child can grow up anxiety free, secure and encased in love, it will never break another child's toy, rip up their paintings or try to scare them. The child will be reliably kind if she or he has reliably been shown kindness.

But experience suggests the existence of some ineluctably dark sides hard-wired in us and beyond the reach of the gentlest behaviour: certain kinds of aggression, cruelty and violence appear to be a given. A child may just want to hit its sibling out of excess vitality, boredom or native sadism. It might just be fun to smack someone in the face to see what happens.

That's why there used to be such an emphasis on manners. Those who upheld them didn't believe that a child ever could be spontaneously good simply because they'd been shown love. Indeed, a firm denial of love was what was necessary to help the child to create a wall between what they might feel inside and what they knew they could express with others. Being strict wasn't a route to making anyone evil, it was a way to teach a person to keep their evil firmly locked up inside themselves.

6. You can't guarantee their success

The modern parent believes that it might be possible to mould a happy, fulfilled, successful human. From this flows the minute attention to detail, from the purchase of the cot to the time-tabling of after-school activities. It is this that explains the Mandarin lessons, the French horn, the educational trips to the countryside and the ruinous tutor fees—because with all this in place, fate and failure can surely be kept at bay.

Yet the relationship between effort and return is more bizarre and more random. We cannot spare those we love the cup of human sorrow—whatever the intensity of our after-school programmes. We are always statistically most likely to give birth to mediocrities.

7. You will be forgotten

You take great care not to be frightening. You make silly jokes, put on funny voices, pretend to be a bear or a camel—all so as not to intimidate, so as to be approachable, the way one's own parents were not. It should be a recipe for reciprocated love.

But weirdly, we rather like difficult people in a way, people we can't quite read, who aren't around so often, who are a bit scary. They hook us in—in a way the kind, stable ones never quite do. One loses authority by being natural, approachable, friendly, a bit daft, the clown who doesn't want to scare.

An even more dispiriting thought comes to mind. Love them reliably and without fear and you will be forgotten. Be distant, intermittent, often absent and deeply volatile, and they will be obsessed with you for life.

And with these thoughts fully aired, it will be time for the kindly parent to attempt to return to sleep. It will be a long day—with the kids—tomorrow.

MORE
With

a
ION
ars
OU

What Did We Do Next?

Sandra Savage

True love is realized in the few short seconds between telling your spouse that you have cancer and his reply is, "what do we do next?"

We.

Not me, not you—but us.

We.

Never did we imagine, standing in front of our priest, holding tightly to each other's hands with all of our family and friends behind us, that "in sickness and in health" meant potentially—ultimately—saying goodbye to the one that you promised to love, honor and cherish you 'till death do you part.

And now the both of us are thinking that our hands, with decades of intertwined hopes, memories and dreams, will be released sooner than later.

Glorious memories of late night whispers, hot tubs and laughter under the full moon, and the fervent make-up sex are soon replaced with nausea, hair loss and days of humiliation and hibernation.

Yet, Michael stays with me. He is putting his employment in jeopardy—and yet, without it, we would hold the total burden of my exhaustive medical expenses.

But I am Michael's priority. And this is a weight on my decimating body.

What I do next is out of love for my husband.

The Sixth Stage of Grief is Retro-computing

Paul Ford

1/10
Emulation Fever

Over the last few days I've been crazy for emulation—that is, simulating old, busted computers on my sweet modern laptop. I've been booting up fake machines and tearing them down, one after the other, and not doing much besides. Machines I've only heard of, arcade games I never played, and programs I never used. Software about which I was always curious. And old favorites like MacWrite.

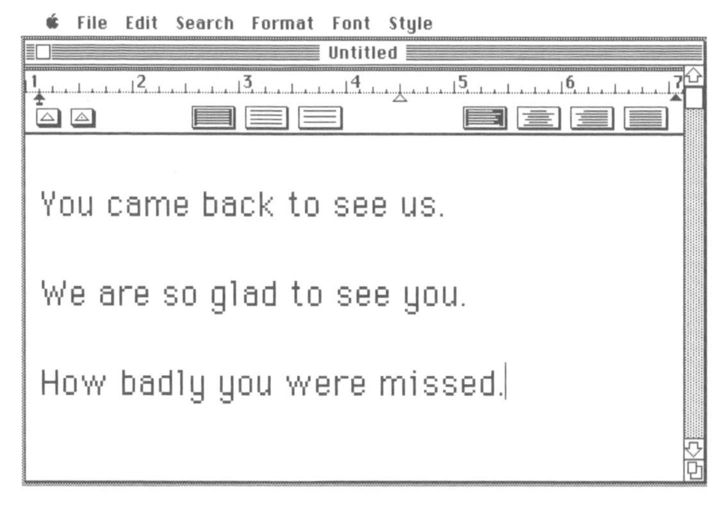

MacWrite on a Macintosh Plus.

Hour after hour, this terrible fever. *What the hell am I doing?* I kept asking myself. *Why am I forcing a fine new machine to pretend it is a half-dozen old, useless machines?*

Eventually I realized: This might be about my friend Tom dying. At least I think so. I am not good at identifying my own motives. It usually takes me at least ten days and a number of snacks to go from feeling something to being able to articulate what I felt. Indeed, I got the news ten days ago, in an email from my friend Jim.

2/10
"Really sad news"

"Really sad news" was the subject. Tom died at 73, after an illness. Here is a picture of him from 1999. He is the one on your left.

Imagine having, in your confused adolescence, the friendship of an older, avuncular man who is into computers, a world-traveling photographer who would occasionally head out to, like, videotape the Dalai Lama for a few weeks, then come back and listen to every word you said while you sat on his porch. A generous, kind person who spoke openly about love and faith and treated people with respect.

We had fallen out of touch. It was good to have known him.

3/10
The Amiga 1000
(What is it good for?)

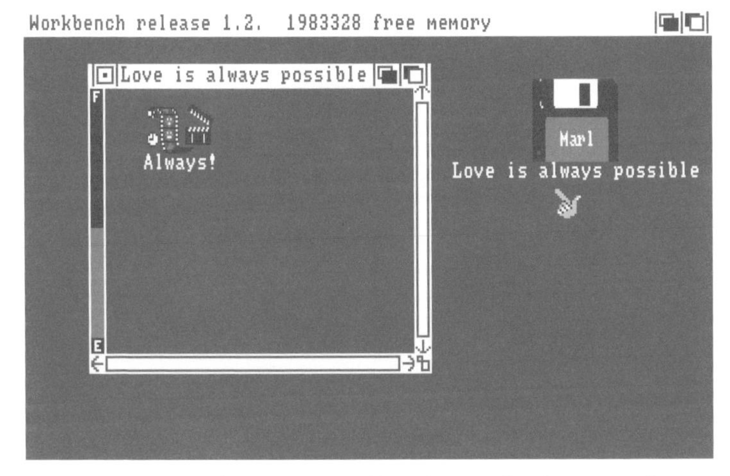

An early version of the Amiga Workbench, a graphical user interface.

I *always* knew Tom. He rented a room from my grandparents. When I was 12, my parents succumbed to my begging and bought me an Amiga computer. By coincidence Tom had one too. Amigas were in the air because we lived near its manufacturer, Commodore, in Pennsylvania.

But the Amiga had a problem. The IBM PC was for *business*; you used it to track stocks and type up reports.

The Apple Macintosh was for *fancy business*, for work done in art galleries or loft apartments. You might use it to publish a newsletter for gourmets who were also physicists.

Amiga 1000 being its beautiful self.

And the Amiga was for... well. It was originally conceived as a videogame console, then the game industry faltered—this was in 1984, when Atari had produced so many excess videogames that it had to bury them in the desert[1] to get rid of them. Commodore bought the Amiga designs in the hopes of competing with the Macintosh.

But Commodore was best known for its "bitty boxes," cheap, popular machines like the VIC-20 and Commodore 64 that sold at Sears. Could it compete?

The Amiga launch event was held in 1985 at Lincoln Center in New York City. A tall man named Robert Pariseau (head of software) emceed, in tuxedo and tremendous ponytail. They enlisted the Amiga to make pie charts, forced it to speak and "multi-task," and made it *become* an IBM PC to run a spreadsheet.

To conclude the night Andy Warhol, in his wig and brightly-colored glasses, came on stage along with Debbie Harry. He used the Amiga to snap a photo of Debbie Harry's face and began to manipulate it live, using a mouse. Debbie Harry sat passively with her eternal pout, but Warhol had fun messing with her hair on the screen. This was a mistake, because both Debbie Harry and Andy Warhol were almost obscenely beautiful. The lovely little machine, juxtaposed with two people who actively epitomized sophistication, couldn't hold its own. The whole thing just seems weird.

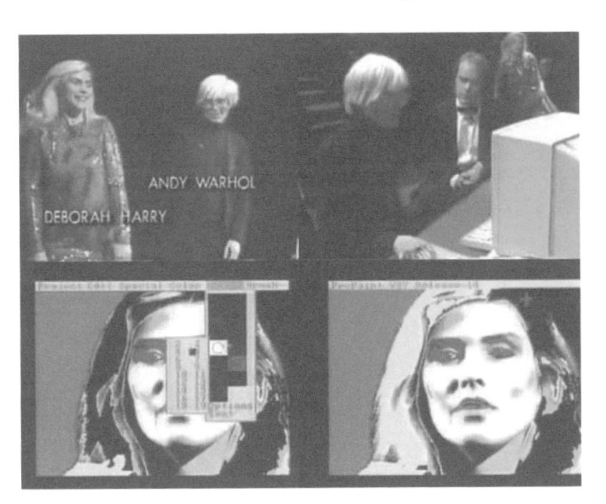

Warhol and Harry at the 1985 Amiga Launch event.

That was the launch. Now they had to sell it to the masses. Here Commodore transformed confusion into bafflement.

"As our TV screen is filled with the computer screen on which appears a wide-eyed fetus," wrote the *New York Times* in 1985[2], describing the first Amiga commercial[3], "the voiceover delivers practically its only line in the 60-second commercial: 'Re-experience the mind unbounded.'"

No one knew what they were doing, so they retreated to gibberish. But it never got better. Consider the stills below from one video in 1987[4]. Take the two-and-a-half minutes to watch it. Let it inside. Be with me in 1987.

So. That's the Amiga. It found niches—it was big in Europe, a favorite of hackers and programmers alike; it was beloved of video producers like my friend Tom. But it never became a true global platform. Microsoft Windows 3 came out in 1990, the beginning of a barely-challenged 20-year ascendancy; Commodore was out of business by 1994.

Like all also-ran underdogs the Amiga inspired a maniacal affection in its users that took decades to exhaust. Here's another still of a video[5] made by an Amiga user in 2000 or later (his screenshot of "OS 3.9" can be used to date the video). Note that he is singing the same song from the 1987 video.

It was fun while it lasted.

4/10
Networks Without Networks

In 1987 my father and I went to the Amiga users' group meetings in nearby Downingtown. These were held in a basement of a computer store with wood paneling. At the users' group you could buy floppy disks for a few bucks, and on them would be items downloaded from local bulletin board systems. Hardly anyone had modems, so this was how files were transmitted. Tom would be at the user group meeting sometimes. Or he'd pick me up and drive me over if my father was busy.

Steve —— 2/17/75

AMATEUR COMPUTER USERS GROUP
HOMEBREW COMPUTER CLUB . . . you name it.

Are you building your own computer? Terminal? T V Typewriter? I/O device? or some other digital black-magic box?

Or are you buying time on a time-sharing service?

If so, you might like to come to a gathering of people with like-minded interests. Exchange information, swap ideas, talk shop, help work on a project, whatever . . .

We are getting together Wednesday nite, March 5th, 7 pm at the home of Gordon French 614 18th Ave., Menlo Park (near Marsh Road).

If you can't make it this time, drop us a card for the next meeting.

See ya there, Fred Moore

Hope you can come.
There will be other Altair builders there.

A 1975 invitation to the legendary Homebrew Computer Club, which birthed the modern home computer industry.

This is how a network comes together. You bought something and then you wanted to understand it, so you went out and found other people. You found them via posters in hallways, or word of mouth, or by purchasing a magazine that caught your eye and then reading the ads in the back.

You'd go to a party and browse through the host's record collection, chat about the album, and maybe decide to go see a concert together—or in some cases you'd start a band.

Another example: Steve Wozniak built the Apple I computer because he knew the people at the Homebrew Computer Club would think it was cool. He wanted to blow their minds, and he did. A lot of times when people talk about Apple, Inc.—one of the largest social and corporate structures in the world, larger than many governments—they talk about design, manufacturing, and vertical integration. But the main driver for Apple's early excellence was that Wozniak wanted to look cool in his little nerd network. He'd show his work to friends and they'd show him what they were working on. Without that, nothing that followed.

Commodore considered buying Apple back when Apple was in a garage. Steve Jobs was interested in selling. It fell through.

5/10
The Nodal Porch

A year after the Amiga showed up—I was 13—my life started to go backwards. Not forever, just for a while. My dad left, money was tight. My clothes were the ones my dad left behind, old blouse-like Oxfords in the days of Hobie Cat surfwear. I was already big and weird, and now I was something else. I think my slide perplexed my peers; if anything they bullied me less. I heard them murmuring as I wandered down the hall.

I was a ghost and I had haunts: I vanished into the computer. I had that box of BBS floppies. One after another I'd insert them into the computer and examine every file, thousands of files all told. That was how I pieced together the world. Second-hand books and BBS disks and trips to the library. I felt very alone but I've since learned that it was a normal American childhood, one millions of people experienced.

Often—how often I don't remember—I'd go over to Tom's. I'd share my techniques for rotating text in Deluxe Paint[6], show him what I'd gleaned from my disks. He always had a few spare computers around for generating title sequences in videos, and later for editing, and he'd let me practice with his videocameras. And he would listen to me.

Still from a Deluxe Paint V animation

Like I said: Avuncular. He wasn't a father figure. Or a mother figure. He was just a kind ear when I needed as many kind ears as I could find. I don't remember what I said; I just remember *being heard*. That's the secret to building a network. People want to be heard. God, life, history, science, books, computers. The regular conversations of anxious kids. His students would show up, impossibly sophisticated 19-year-old men and women, and I'd listen to them talk as the sun went down. For years. A world passed over that porch and I got to watch and participate even though I was still a boy.

I constantly apologized for being there, for being so young and probably annoying, and people would just laugh at me. But no one put me in my place. People touched me, hugged me, told me about books to read and movies to watch. I was not a ghost.

When I graduated from high school I went by to sit on the porch and Tom gave me a little brown teddy bear. You need to remember, he said, to be a kid. To stay in touch with that part of yourself.

I did not do this.

6/10
General Instructions on How to Emulate

Emulating is a nerdy hobby that takes an enormous amount of time. If you enjoy reading manuals for spreadsheet programs from 1983, you'll love software emulation. (If your eyes glaze over at the thought, just skip a page.)

You typically need four things to emulate an old computer:

1. The emulator software.
This lets your computer pretend it is a different kind of computer. It can range from commercial tools like

VMWare Fusion[7] which allows you to emulate a Windows PC on a Mac, to things like MAME[8], which pretends to be every kind of arcade machine, or VICE[9], which emulates the early Commodore computers. You can also buy emulators, like Amiga Forever[10] or C64 Forever[11]. Buying things means it's all done for you and you can ignore the steps that follow.

2. The ROM files.

There's a liminal kind of software called the BIOS, or Basic Input/Output System. This is the nervous system of a computer; it's what's already installed even before a computer starts to load its operating system. For most systems some enterprising nerd has pulled the ROMS out of hardware and given them a name like KXK1CFJ.ROM. These files are almost always copyrighted, so to find them you have to Google around for things like "mac plus ROM" and wade through a lot of weird hedging language to find what you need. Just look for phrases like: "You cannot download this file unless you own a ColecoVision Model X Grobbler Frog Controller" followed by a big blue link to the file you cannot download, that you must never download. The entire world of emulation is filled with references to very specific things that you should not seek out, that you must never Google, that you should definitely not obtain.

3. An operating system.

Once you have the emulator and the ROM it's like you actually own a new, old, computer—but it lacks for an operating system. Want to experience System 6.08 for your Mac? Workbench 2 for the Amiga? Microsoft DOS 6.22? You'll likely make a fake hard drive. Then you actually *install* the real, authentic operating system onto the fake hard drive.

Sometimes you will need to "insert" fake "floppy disks" into the fake "floppy drive" in order to install the real operating system onto the fake "hard drive" on the fake "computer." (This is accomplished by clicking buttons.) Then you'll "reboot." It's all very weird.

4. Software.
You might luck out and find a virtual hard drive pre-loaded with hundreds of applications; then you can download that whole bad boy and just coast. I've got one for the Mac, it's 542 megabytes of joy. Want to use Photoshop 1.0 in black and white with German-language menus? No? Well, I do. More likely you will need to download virtual disks. You can find these by searching around for the word "abandonware" plus the name of the operating system you like. Sometimes you will find lovingly tended sites like Macintosh Garden[12]. There are also the TOSEC collections[13], which have tens of thousands of archived computer programs to choose from; just about *every* Amiga program is available. In general, abandonware websites are badly categorized nightmares that require you to click five affiliate links to download a 20 kilobyte DOS file—or hyper-categorized massive sets of tens of thousands of disks created by obsessive completists. Either way, whoa.

The world of retro-computing is scattered, chaotic, murky, and legally suspect—although major progress is being made by the Internet Archive[14], among other organizations, at bringing old software into the light. To my knowledge, no one has ever been prosecuted for downloading twenty-year-old word processing software.

Good luck.

7/10
Reunion

Last week my friend Jim emailed:

> And all the Amiga memories. Man oh man. We'd trade equipment and software. He had a name for it: let's "play 'puters" he'd say. That's Tom too. We were always hitting each other up for software. Wrote many a long serial number down for him.

In 2002, Jim and Tom and I got together and went down to an Amiga festival at a hotel in Maryland. It was—even by the standards of nerd events—well, it was rough. Men had Amiga logos woven into their beards. People with ailments sold disks out of worn cardboard boxes. I had expected it to be like an alumni weekend, a chance to get together and chat about old times. But these people were angry. I remember driving back and feeling stupefied. How could all that sweetness have leached from the world? I blamed Microsoft Windows.

But that was wrong. In truth, there was nothing to blame. Companies come and companies go and things turn out differently than you'd hope.

That's the last long stretch of time I spent with Tom.

I don't know why I drifted. He never took to email. I wanted distance from my family, from my childhood. I still know his phone number by heart. At least once a month I'd think of calling. Of going down for a visit.

We kept very loose tabs on each other through our mutual friend Jim. Using that oldest of networks, people talking about each other.

8/10
Selections from My Week of Emulations

Here is a late-1970s vintage Xerox Alto running Bravo:

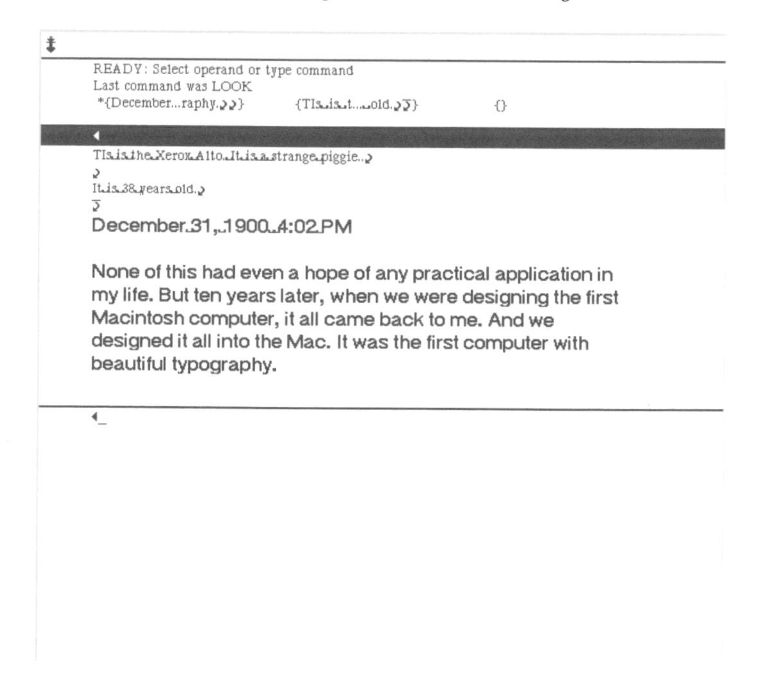

The machine was a Xerox Alto. The word processor was called Bravo. The software is from 1976 or a year or two later—hard to tell—although the quote I typed in is from Steve Jobs in 2005. The Alto had a command line and no icons but used a mouse with three buttons. It also featured drawing programs and games and was typically plugged into a network. It was created to serve the needs of a research community, to bind them together and give them a common language with which to express ideas about technology. It cost more than a house.

Here is an early version of MacOS running on a Mac Plus, circa 1986:

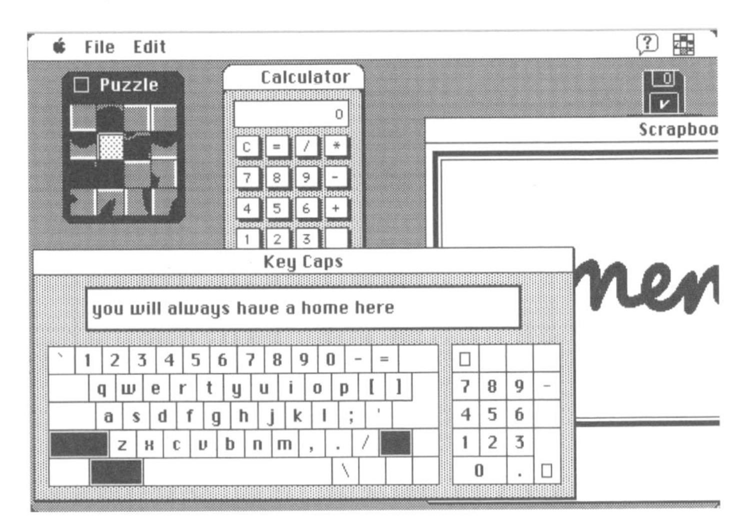

The Mac did not invent that much—but do we criticize Giorgio Armani for not inventing the suit? It turned the inside of the computer into a place with warm little windows. It was expensive and a little snobby—like a nice mint-green polo shirt with a little black alligator embossed above your heart. It saw mass, popular computing not as a set of commands, but as an ongoing, continual experience. That people are so eager to share that experience, how urgent and real it can feel to them, is why Apple is so unbelievably huge today.

Here is a Macintosh Plus running Smalltalk-80, 1987:

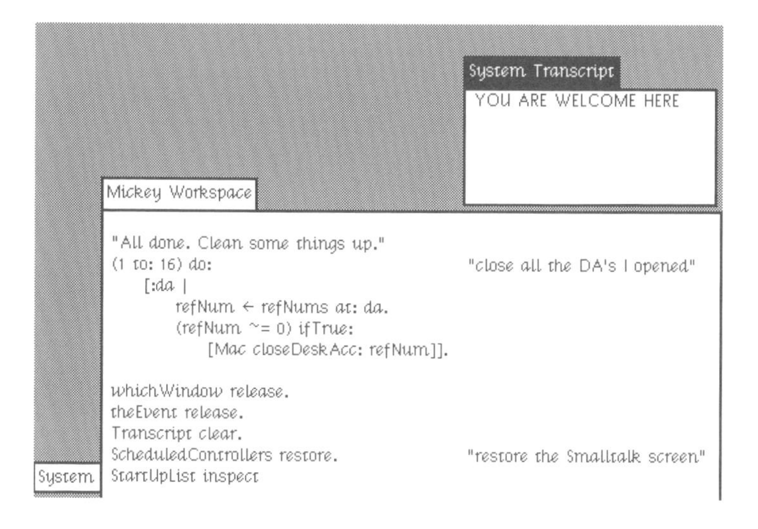

This is a Mac too, but it's running Smalltalk-80. Smalltalk was a product of the Xerox Alto culture, and was created along with the Alto. It was where many of the current ideas that are prevalent in computing—object-oriented coding, windowing systems, and graphics—were first refined into usable software products.

When the Mac people went over to study what Xerox was doing, they were copying Smalltalk ideas. (Adele Goldberg, one of the co-creators of Smalltalk, refused to show Steve Jobs the system, until her bosses gave express permission. Which they did. Apple was paying to see.)

Smalltalk-80 is a kind of programming language but you don't run programs independently; rather, you open up large-ish "image files" that are themselves a kind of virtual machine—so here we are emulating a Mac and then running another fake computer, in the form of the Small-talk virtual machine, atop it.

In 2014, Smalltalk is an idea that keeps going, in the form of a programming environment called Squeak[15], and in other versions, too. The idea of the Mac keeps going too. The Alto keeps going in the form of windows and good fonts. This is important to me, that sense of continuity. The typical story of technology is one of progress; your floppies get old and decrepit and you can't see your old data, that's basically your fault, and who wants to live in the past? But human networks often stick around for decades, half-centuries. People have been working on Smalltalk for more than 40 years, for as long as I have been alive. Just continually thinking about it, how to improve it, how to make it popular, how to get the world to acknowledge it. It binds them together. I respect that.

Here is an Amiga running TextCraft, its first word processor, which cost $99.95 in 1987:

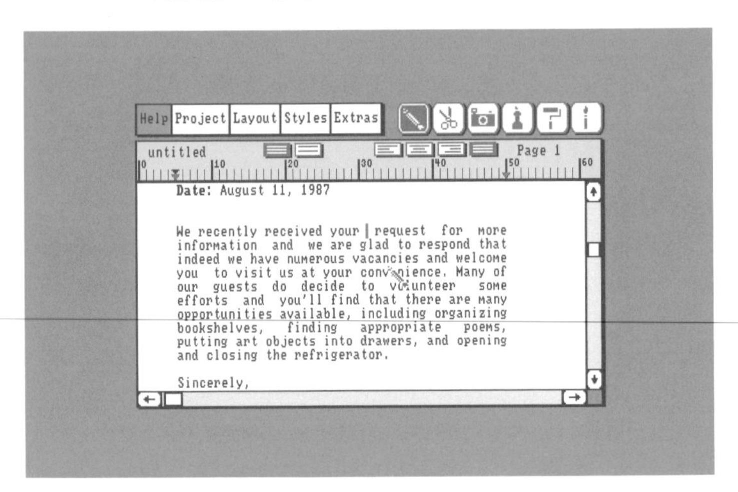

I spent hours here, sorting my young thoughts. Even back in 1987 we knew this program was an ugly disaster. Note the use of a little mucilage jar for... pasting. Programs like WordStar or WordPerfect were much, much better, but they only ran on MS-DOS back then. Or more obscure operating systems like CP/M. So we worked with what we had and we talked about it and made do.

Here is a recent installation of Plan 9, a descendant of Unix created in the 1990s

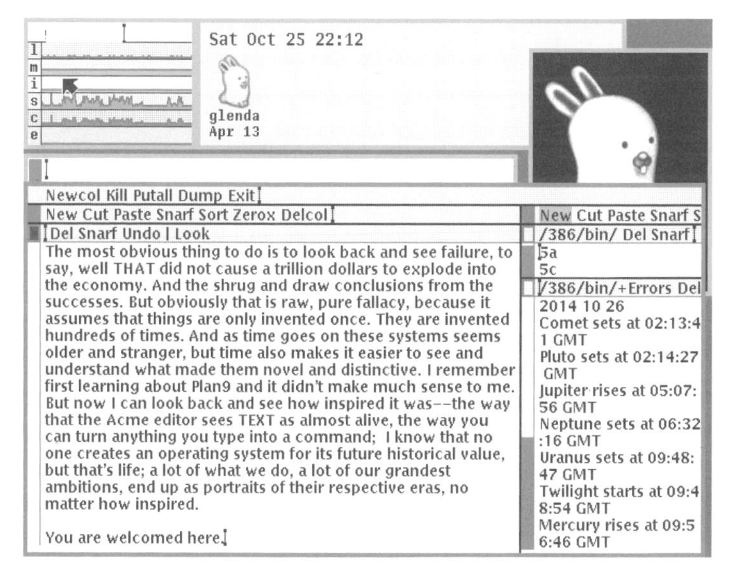

Plan 9 is a strange one. Here it is running its window manager, Rio. (Its logo is a rabbit named Glenda.) The Acme text editor, shown above, is a major part of the Plan 9 OS and is a whole world unto itself. Everything in Acme, including the menus, is pure, editable text. This seems very light and easy but the more you think about it the weirder it gets.

I don't know exactly why I ran this operating system during my binge. It came around in the 1990s as a possible successor to Unix. It did not become the successor to Unix, but the ideas within it are reinvented, in a debased and half-considered form, about once an hour in the open source community.

Here is an Emulated LISP Machine running OpenGenera from the 90s

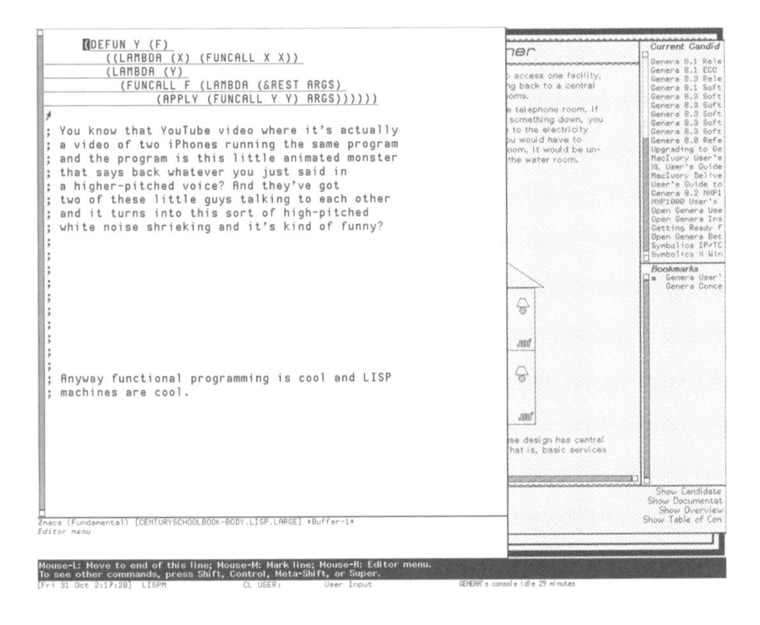

The reason I was running a Lisp machine is that it represents this very specific vision of technology, where computers were deeply powerful and infinitely customizable and incredibly easy to manipulate.

LISP is a computer language. But for a period in the 1980s there were Lisp machines: A computer that was all in a single language, from its weirdest inner parts to its windows and mouse cursor. Everything unified, pure, and open to inspection and manipulation.

What you see here is not a Lisp machine per se, but a Lisp machine simulator designed to run atop a Unix system—like Smalltalk atop the Mac.

It is a very weird experience. It feels like a machine for monks or nuns. Baffling. But there is this weird sense of raw power, like you have been handed the keys to a nuclear-powered submarine. It might take you a few months or years to learn the mysteries. That's fine. LISP won't change.

Smalltalk was deeply inspired by the LISP language. Everything was deeply inspired by LISP, because it's so fundamental. People either learned it, and were inspired, or refused to learn it, and reinvented it in half-assed form.

Here is a Windows 3.1 Machine running Microsoft Paint, circa 1992

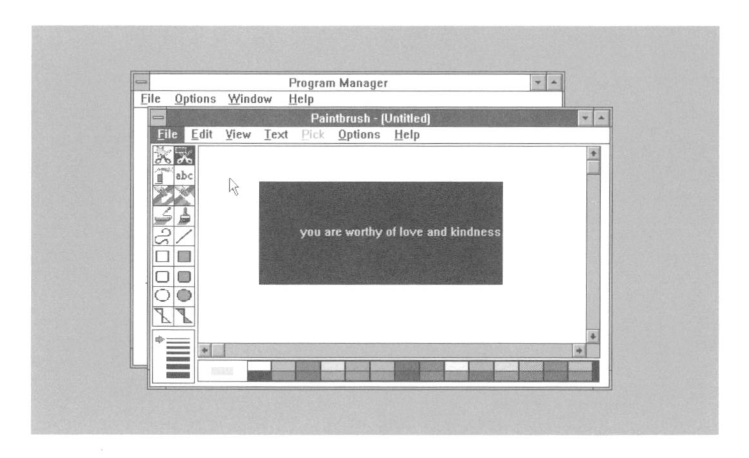

This is Windows. It is a layer above an operating system called MS-DOS. It was made by a company in Seattle. It changed the world economy by being all things to all people. You can no longer be all things to all people when it comes to computers, but Microsoft keeps trying. Windows is an accurate representation of what people expect from computers, which on one hand is fascinating and the other is a tragedy.

It really worked for tens of millions of people and changed their computing lives. And there was some wonderful software that resulted. That said: Windows is the Superbowl Halftime Show of operating systems. Given what everyone got paid, and how many people were involved, you'd think it would be more memorable.

Here is a NeXT OpenStep Environment Running Interface Builder, circa 1997

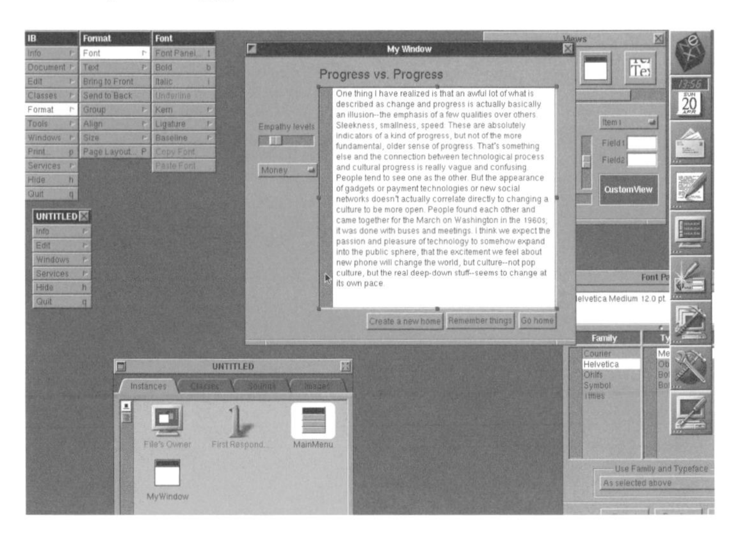

This last one, the NeXT machine, is complicated. I never had a NeXT machine, but NeXT machines haunt our world. Like Lisp machines, like Smalltalk, their users were incredibly vociferous excited people who talked about using them in almost religious tones.

The difference is that NeXT's OS went from being a somber lesson about being too ambitious to being one of the dominant operating systems in the world, and everyone *still* talks about it in religious tones.

I guess I need to explain.

9/10
Steve Jobs on and off Typography

In his commencement speech at Stanford University in 2005, Steve Jobs described taking a calligraphy course as an undergraduate at Reed College in Oregon. "I learned about serif and sans-serif typefaces, about varying the amount of space between different letter combinations, about what makes great typography great." He went on:

> None of this had even a hope of any practical application in my life. But ten years later, when we were designing the first Macintosh computer, it all came back to me. And we designed it all into the Mac. It was the first computer with beautiful typography.

Yesterday I booted up the emulator for the Xerox Alto. The Alto was arguably the first modern general-purpose computer—a big screen, modern software, and you used a mouse to point. It was never generally available but it was the Velvet Underground of computers, in that everyone who saw it went on to make their own computer industry. As I wrote above, when Apple went to Xerox to license its technology for MacOS, it was copying ideas that had been created on Alto computers.

When you boot up the Xerox Alto the fonts are right there, listed: Helvetica was a first-class citizen of that operating system, many years before that first Mac pinged awake.

After he was fired from Apple, Jobs went off and built NeXT. The NeXT computer was a hodgepodge: Bits of Alto, from Xerox research; bits of UNIX from Bell Labs, the research arm of the giant US telephone monopoly. Its core language, Objective C, was an unholy union of Xerox "object oriented" approaches and the Bell Labs "C" programming language. They also built a tool to ease the programmer's labors—a software development tool called Interface Builder. That started as a government-funded project in France, was turned into a feature of a version of the LISP programming language that ran on Macintoshes, and then found its way to the Mac. Its direct descendant is what you use today to build iPhone apps.

Many roads going back through computing history lead back to Steve Jobs, or pause along the way at his office. But they don't stop there. They go back to INRIA's labs in France, back to Bell Labs in New Jersey, MIT in Massachusetts, back to Xerox's Palo Alto Research Center—a surprisingly short drive from One Infinite Loop, Apple's headquarters in Cupertino.

And further back still: To people reviewing each other's album collections, back to the post office, the railway systems, radio networks, sporting events. People building roads. Networks are natural things.

In their day NeXT systems were seen as insanely expensive, bordering on pretentious; they were never intended for the masses but had a strong focus on the academic market. NeXT looked down on the world of popular computing from a very high window; meanwhile, Windows sold hot dogs on the street. ("Write software for it?" said Bill Gates of the NeXT. "I'll piss on it.")

You can do good work in high towers. The World Wide Web was bootstrapped on a NeXT machine. The videogame "Doom" was written on NeXTs. And famously, Apple bought NeXT in 1997 for $400 million ($50 million of that in debt), and just as famously Jobs began to overtake Apple, to make it his own again. It was not smooth. When they turned NeXTStep into MacOSX people were baffled. They made videos to complain—years before YouTube, videos that you had to download or stream from random websites over slow connections. A friend downloaded one of our favorites[16] so that we could watch it together on his laptop.

The organized environment of MacOS9 was being taken away. We'd all been moved to a new house in the middle of the night. *What is this? Why did they change it? What is it for?* It wasn't clear. Because of the iPod and iTunes, Apple was now discussed as a music and entertainment company that also did computers. What was this? What was it for?

Then came the iPhone. At first there was no App Store, no way to run your code within it, and people railed and gnashed their teeth. But then there was an App Store. The way you built apps was with Objective C and the Interface Builder. No other approach was permitted. There was gnashing of teeth, but less so. Not only was the NeXT ideology successful, but it was enforced. Aligning yourself with its methods was the price one paid to participate in an enormous cultural landrush. Today Apple is worth 1,000 times as much money as it paid for NeXT. "Good artists copy," Jobs once said, misattributing it to Picasso. "Great artists steal." Perhaps a more accurate statement would have been: *Great popularizers license.*

When people get rich it always ends up sounding like destiny. And the actual narratives sound too small, too fragile—and impossible to reproduce. Which makes for a bad story. Good stories are ones you can learn from. Imagine standing in front of the graduating class of Stanford and saying,

> Man, I don't know. Wozniak wanted to show off for his nerd friends. I was ready to sell to Commodore. Xerox was so focused on the 1990s they forgot about the 1980s. NeXT just got further and further into the quagmire. Pixar, before Toy Story, was the only hardware company less successful than NeXT. The iPhone launched without an App Store. But people were drawn to me, and I told them what they needed to hear in order to make each other rich. So do that: Go out there and tell people what they need to hear in order to make each other rich. When something works say that was the plan all along.

That would be a terrible commencement speech.

10/10
Technology is What We Share

Technology is what we share. I don't mean "we share the experience of technology." I mean: By my lights, people very often share *technologies* with each other when they talk. Strategies. Ideas for living our lives. We do it all the time. Parenting email lists share strategies about breast-feeding and bedtime. Quotes from the Dalai Lama. We talk neckties, etiquette, and Minecraft, and tell stories that give us guidance as to how to live. A tremendous part of daily life regards the exchange of technologies. We are good at it. It's so simple as to be invisible. *Can I borrow your scissors? Do you want tickets? I know guacamole is*

extra. The world of technology isn't separate from regular life. It's made to seem that way because of, well... capitalism. Tribal dynamics. Territoriality. Because there is a need to sell technology, to package it, to recoup the terrible investment. So it becomes this thing that is separate from culture. A product.

I went looking for the teddy bear that Tom had given me, the reminder to be a child sometimes, and found it atop a bookshelf. When I pulled it down I was surprised to find that it was in a tiny diaper.

I stood there, ridiculous, a 40-year-old man with a diapered 22-year-old teddy bear in my hand. It stared back at me with root-beer eyes.

This is what I remembered right then: That before my wife got pregnant we had been trying for kids for years without success. We had considered giving up.

That was when I said to my wife: If we do not have children, we will move somewhere where there is a porch. The children who need love will find the porch. They will know how to find it. We will be as much parents as we want to be.

And when she got pregnant with twins we needed the right-sized doll to rehearse diapering. I went and found that bear in an old box.

I was sitting on Tom's porch in 1992 when he handed me that toy. A person offering another person a piece of advice. Life passed through that object as well, through the teddy bear as much as through the operating systems of yore.

Now that I have children I can see how tuned they are to the world. Living crystals tuned to all manner of frequencies. And how urgently they need to be heard. They peer up and they say, look at me. And I put my phone away.

And when they go to bed, protesting and yowling before conking out, I go to mess with my computers, my old weird imaginary emulated computers. System after system. I open up these time capsules and look at the thousands of old applications, millions of dollars of software, but now it can be downloaded in a few minutes and takes up a tiny portion of a hard drive. It's all comically antiquated.

Moore's law, the speed at which technology moves forward, means that the digital past gets smaller every year. What is left are the tracings of hundreds of people, or thousands, who, 20, 30, 40 years ago found each other and decided to fabricate all this digital stuff. This glittering ephemera. They left these markings and moved on. Looking at the emulated machines feels... big, somehow. Like standing at a Grand Canyon with a river of bright green pixels running along the bottom.

When you read oral histories of technology, whether of successes or failures, you sense the yearning of people who want to get back into those rooms for a minute, back to solving the old problems. How should the mouse look? What will people want to do, when we give them these machines? How should a window open? Who wouldn't want to go back 20 years—to drive again into the office, to sit before the whiteboard in a beanbag chair, in a place of warmth and clarity, and give it another try?

Such a strange way to say goodbye. So here I am. Imaginary disks whirring and screens blinking as I visit my old haunts. Wandering through lost computer worlds for an hour or two, taking screenshots like a tourist. Shutting one virtual machine down with a sigh, then starting up another one. But while these machines run, I am a kid. A boy on a porch, back among his friends.

—

1. en.wikipedia.org/wiki/Atari_video_game_burial
2. nyti.ms/1MVeAjp
3. youtu.be/8ZiWTdc6Dc8
4. youtu.be/PWeO5IkCssk
5. youtu.be/tNti5bN9ILU
6. en.wikipedia.org/wiki/Deluxe_Paint
7. vmware.com/products/fusion
8. mamedev.org
9. vice-emu.sourceforge.net
10. amigaforever.com
11. c64forever.com
12. macintoshgarden.org
13. archive.org/details/tosec
14. archive.org/details/internetarcade
15. squeak.org
16. youtu.be/-xUHuXgySO8

Neon

Hannah Fletcher

I sat beneath the buzzing neon sign and let its reverberations break through the dream. I determined that I would never come back—to this seat by the window, to the untouched curry on the table, to the boy. We talked for too long and in broken sentences, until finally I was just a small voice saying "okay" and biking off in the dark. Back at home, I laid on my bed in my shoes and cried. In those brief moments, the last three years flooded me and left in an instant.

Something shifted shortly after that. I can't say what exactly changed or when the page turned. As with all growth, it happened inexplicably and imperceptibly. And on one Friday, busing back into the city, I felt a completeness and an energy and a readiness for the next pop of light.

First,

Stéphanie Verge

the End

When my mother told me she was leaving my father, we were sitting in an Ottawa food court. The fluorescent light was bouncing off the fluorescent pad thai in front of her.

My first thought: *Finally.*

My second: *In less than two hours I have to be at a wedding, but Mom is crying in the middle of the St. Laurent Shopping Centre. And I still haven't bought a slip.*

—

The first boy my mother ever loved joined the seminary and broke her heart.

My father—then eighteen, with Buddy Holly glasses and a sad past—came next. Four years later, wearing a man's suit and a child's grin, he married my mother, an auburn-haired, gap-toothed sylph. This was his chance. He was taking it.

The first girl I ever loved leaned back against a stone fireplace in a ski chalet in southern Ontario and stole my heart.

She kept it for the next four years and, in a way that pioneers often do, forever.

The summer I was born, my parents were thirty years old. They were setting up a new life in a new town.

The summer I turned thirty, they were setting up new, separate lives in new, separate towns. They came to my party and stared at each other across a backyard filled with my friends.

—

My mother has perfect fingers. Straight and slender, they are relentlessly elegant.

For her entire working life, a ruby engagement ring encircled one of those faultless digits, winking at students from the blackboard. When my parents got married, a gold band—matching my father's—encircled another.

Dad rarely wore his ring—it was prone to breaking and after a while he stopped getting it repaired. Mom wore hers until the day she didn't.

At some point in the early nineties, my parents had the ruby appraised. It turned out to be a fake in a beautiful antique silver setting: two pieces of glass fused together, the truth only visible under microscope.

I wanted to believe that because my mother had loved the ring, it had value, but the whole thing seemed like a warning against scrutiny.

My girlfriend has perfect fingers too.

The summer I turned thirty-two, that thought kept me company through Arizona and New Mexico, past 2,700 kilometres of mountains and deserts, scrub oaks and adobe homes.

On the Turquoise Trail, I bought a silver ring (certification of authenticity available) and tucked both it and the thought away.

—

When my mother told me she was petitioning to annul her thirty-eight-year marriage to my father, we were sitting in an Indian restaurant in downtown Toronto. I was breaking pieces of pappadum into smaller pieces.

The reason for the request was a poorly kept family secret—Mom's a devout Catholic while Dad's a devout homosexual—but I was still somehow, distantly, shocked. Watching her set a Vatican-approved dissolution in motion gave me a low-grade buzz, like the faint vibration in your fingers after running a vacuum.

I hold vacuum hands responsible for what followed.

Two Things I Know Now That I Didn't Know Then, When I Proposed to My Long-Distance Girlfriend of Six Months

1. Though an unabashed believer in True Love and Big Romantic Gestures, my long-distance girlfriend of six months had a healthy suspicion of a marriage proposal that came on the heels of an annulment announcement, even if the ring did, in fact, travel to her all the way from New Mexico.

2. Though an unabashed believer in Clear-Headed Behaviour, I failed to make a connection between an annulment announcement and a marriage proposal, even when pressed, in favour of proselytizing about The One, a concept I historically abhorred.

—

We made it past the six-month mark. She took the ring, but clarified that in no way did this mean we were engaged. (She sensed that the proposal was sincere and likely to resurface.)

We made it six months further and another six months after that.

She spent summer holidays, winter breaks, and reading weeks in Toronto, grading papers. I spent weekends with her in Montreal, eating croissants.

She met my father's boyfriend and my mother's boyfriend. Together, we watched my parents attempt to ease into a friendship based on the same thing that had held them together—the children—then renege ("too soon," my mother would say).

We would talk about marriage but it always ended in an argument. Me, insisting, she, backing away ("too soon," she'd say). Anxious for reciprocity, I stopped asking.

After a stack of six-month chunks, I quit my job and moved to Montreal, to the neighbourhood where my parents lived as newlyweds. My mother and father visited separately, but told us the same stories of life there together. They spoke only of the happy times.

And on one otherwise unremarkable day, my girlfriend started talking about marriage.

—

The morning we eloped, I sent my parents flowers. The same message in both bouquets, in case they compared notes: “We have good news. Stay by the phone.”

Our vows weren’t about what came easy: love and faithfulness. They were about the importance of family, the meaning of respect, the value of empathy.

They were about the end of one marriage and the beginning of another.

This was our chance. And we were taking it.

LOVE IS
REPETITIOUS

DISTANCE OPTIONS

1. out of sight, out of mind.

2. distance makes the heart grow fonder.

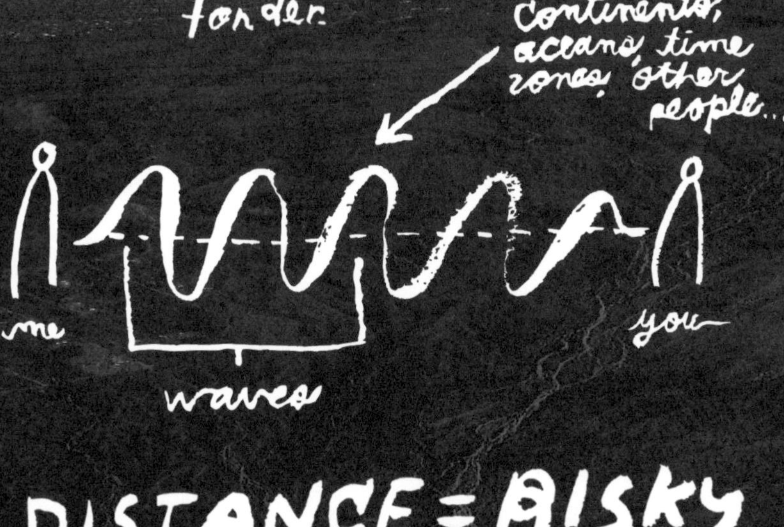

continents, oceans, time zones, other people...

me

you

waves

DISTANCE = RISKY.

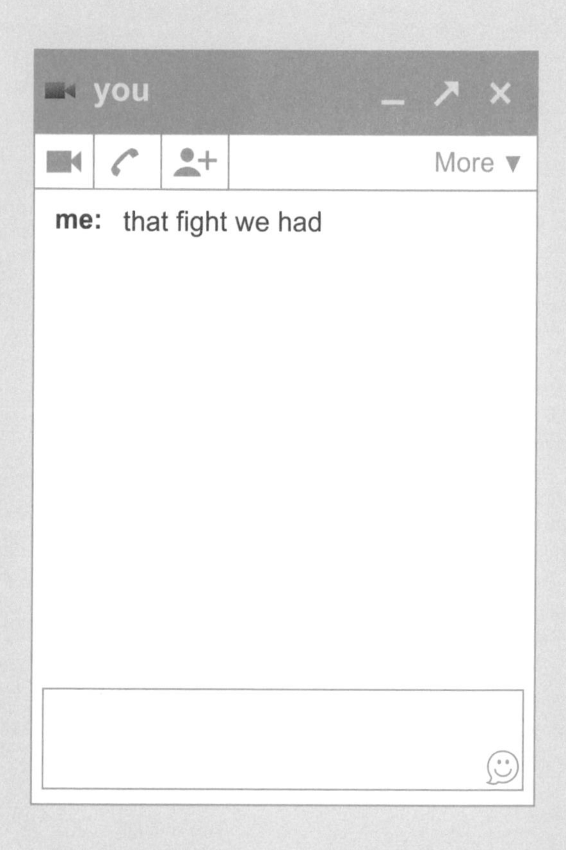
you
More ▼
me: that fight we had

you

More ▼

me: that fight we had

you are typing...

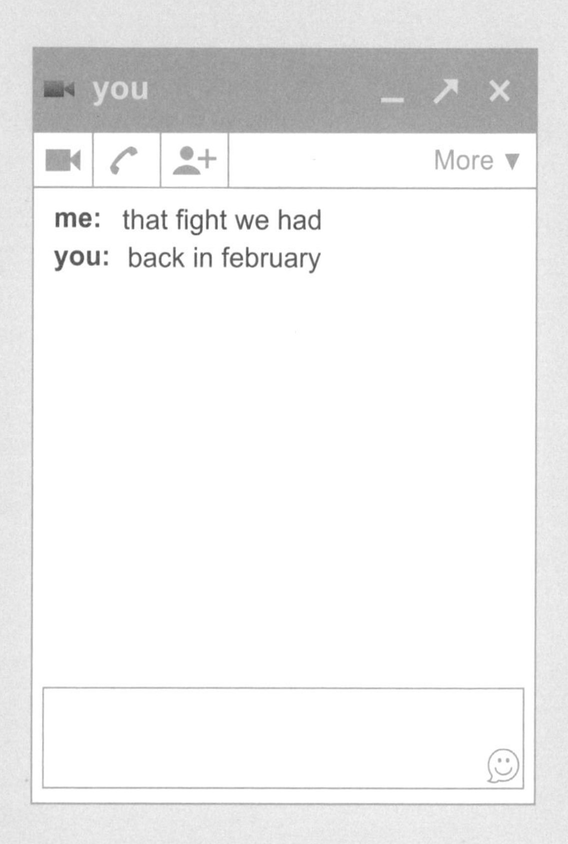
you
More ▼
me: that fight we had
you: back in february

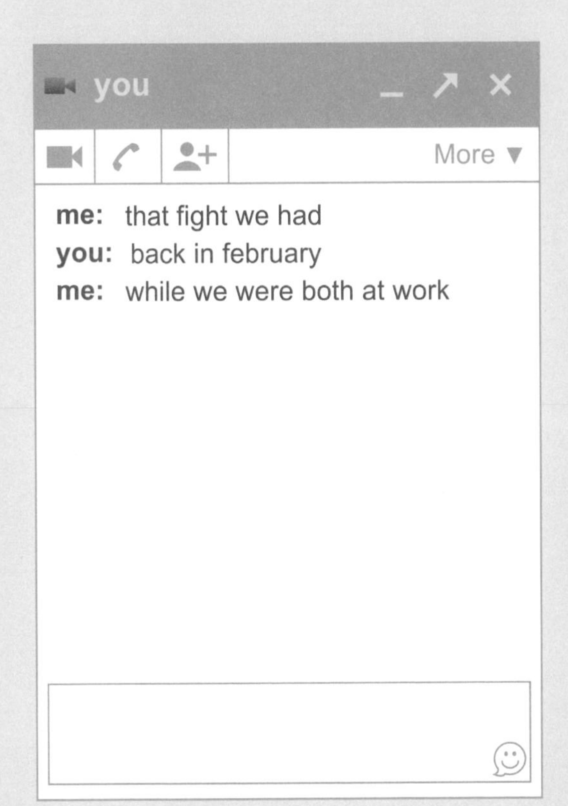
you
More ▼
me: that fight we had
you: back in february
me: while we were both at work

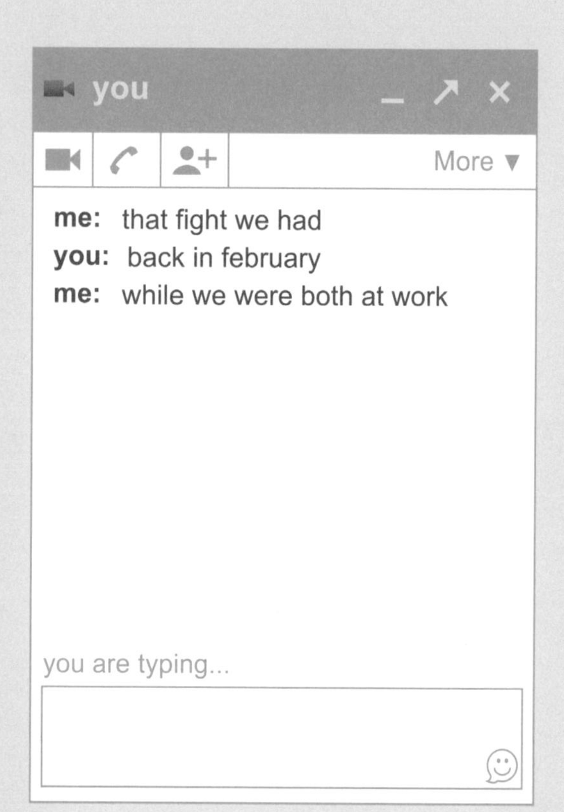
you
More ▼
me: that fight we had
you: back in february
me: while we were both at work
you are typing...

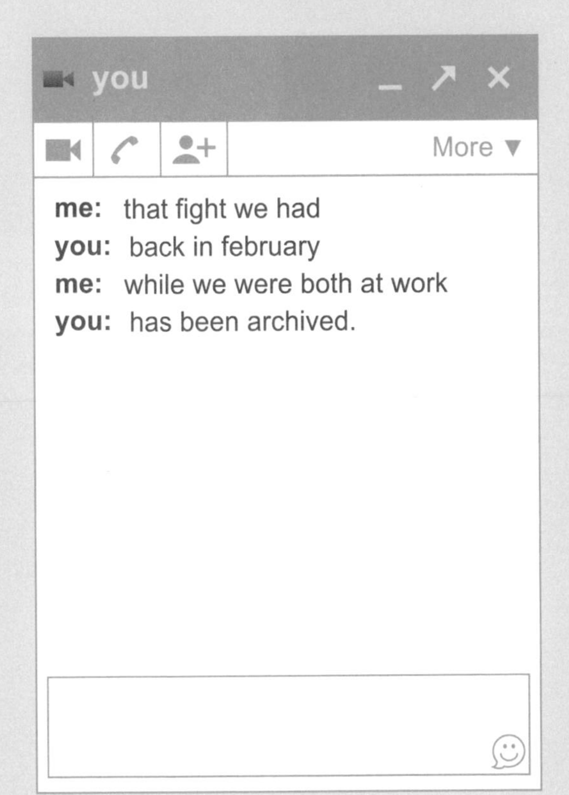
you
More ▼
me: that fight we had
you: back in february
me: while we were both at work
you: has been archived.

Head,

Heart

Lydia Davis

Heart weeps.
Head tries to help heart.
Head tells heart how it is, again.
You will lose the ones you love. They will all go. But even the earth will go, someday.
Heart feels better, then.
But the words of the head do not remain long in the ears of the heart.
Heart is so new to this.
I want them back, says heart.
Head is all heart has.
Help, head. Help heart.

Important Artifacts and Personal Property from the Collection of Lenore Doolan and Harold Morris, Including Books, Street Fashion, and Jewelry

Leanne Shapton

At first glance, Leanne Shapton's *Important Artifacts and Personal Property...* looks like any auction catalog. Each page is filled with items for sale, photographed plainly in black and white with accompanying descriptions and lot numbers. Furniture, fine art, jewelry—all the usual items you might expect are here, but among them are stranger lots—half of a wishbone, a stuffed squirrel, a set of novelty salt and pepper shakers.

Shapton's book is that rare thing: A truly unique breakup story. Her fictional love affair, from secretive beginning to inevitable end, is told through the physical by-products of a relationship—handwritten notes, mix CDs, shared tshirts, goofy photographs, invitations, and well-thumbed books. *Important Artifacts and Personal Property...* tells an intimate story through an oblique lens, punctuated by totems and tchotchkes, and lets us fill in the spaces between. It is briefly excerpted here, but can and should be enjoyed in full at your local library or bookstore.

LOT 1172

A travel clock

An Elgin travel clock, including original box. Given to Morris by Doolan.

$40–60

Doolan insisted that the clock remain on New York time. Morris took the clock on two trips, but complained that it was too heavy.

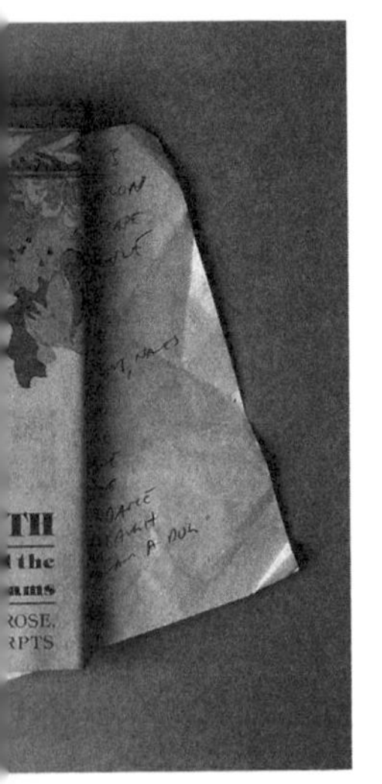

LOT 1173

Plath, Sylvia

Johnny Panic and the Bible of Dreams (Harper & Row, 1978), first edition. Good condition. Laid into the short story "The Fifty-ninth Bear," page 105, is a scrap of yellow foolscap paper with a short handwritten list in Doolan's hand: *"Batteries / Scotch tape / watermelon / Guacamole / Pros: / travel / talk of family, names / Cons: / insensitive / defensive / doesn't dance / fake laugh? / doesn't want a dog."* 9½ x 6½ x 1⅛ in. (book); 8 x 6 in. (note).

$20–45

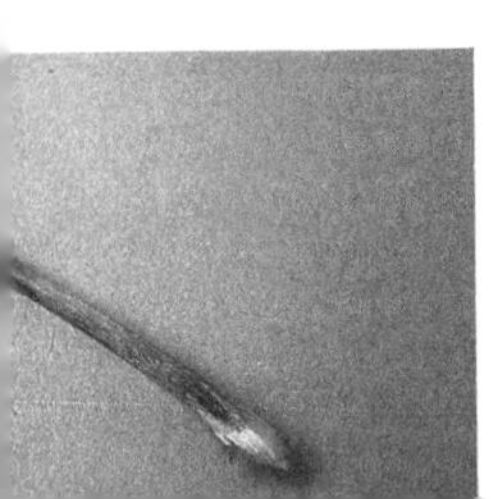

LOT 1174

A half a wishbone

The winning side of a turkey wishbone. Kept by Morris in his bedside table. Length 3½ in.

$5–10

1169

1170

LOT 1169

An invitation

An invitation to a Halloween party, October 31, 2004, given by Morris's close friends Rekha Subramanian and Paulo Vitale. 5¼ x 4 in.

$5–10

Included in lot is a snapshot of Doolan and Morris in Halloween costumes. Doolan is dressed as Anna Magnani, Morris as Paddington Bear. Photographer unknown. 4 x 6 in.

LOT 1170

A blue vase

A blue vase, engraved with signature "McCoy USA." Given by Morris to Doolan, with roses, as an anniversary present (chips and losses). Height 9 in.

$40–55

Doolan later noted in her diary that the roses did not open.

LOT 1171

A pair of cufflinks an

A pair of airplane cufflir
Thanksgiving 2004. Acc
reading: *"Favorite Momen*
into the closet to spare me.
door even though you were
4. When you called the ma
switched places with me at
face." 6 x 3½ in.

Not illustrated.

$10–20

1092

LOT 1092

A group of six bathing suits

One black string bikini, label reading "Triumph International Soleil." One sixties mod print cutout, no label. One brown halter-neck, label reading "Eres." One pink, olive green, red, and yellow stripe, no label. One red bandeau, label reading "APC." One white fifties one-piece, label reading "Sea Queen."

$15–40 (6)

Included in lot is a picture of Doolan wearing white Sea Queen one-piece. The photograph was taken at the Orient Point rental house that Morris shared with friends Jason Frank, Toby Cwir, and Cwir's girlfriend, Alicia Diaz. 4 x 6 in.

1093

1094

LOT 1093

A framed photograph

A framed black-and-white photograph of Morris surfing. Photographer unknown. 8½ x 6½ in.

$15–20

LOT 1094

A group photograph

A color photograph of Morris, Cwir, Frank, Doolan, and Diaz playing Trivial Pursuit at Orient Point. 4 x 6 in.

$15–20

LOT 1095

A group of tag-sale finds

A hardcover book titled *Adventures with Hal*, by Gladys Baker Bond (Whitman, 1965). A bisque bust of Niobe. Five assorted dinner plates.

$10–30 (7)

LOT 1096

A group of maps

Maps from a road trip to Guelph, Ontario, to visit Doolan's family. Dimensions vary.

Not illustrated.

$15–25 (3)

1095

Looking for

Love

Nicolas Burrows

Tomorrow is the first day of the most amazing time in your life!

I will be there for 8—and then we will get in the shower and then the whole process of getting to know about our relationship is going to happen. Afterwards I was thinking maybe we can grab a sandwich and then we could head off on holiday.

Japan?
How about a child?

If you're interested let me know. I'm a musician, I have no problems with my own life and I can see! You can get in contact with me on Twitter.

My name is Mr A.

—

Written in collaboration with the predictive text feature on a Samsung Galaxy III Mini GT18190N.

"LOVE IS NOT IDEALIZATION.
EVERY TRUE LOVER KNOWS THAT IF
YOU REALLY LOVE A WOMAN
OR A MAN THAT YOU DON'T IDEALIZE
HIM OR HER. LOVE MEANS THAT YOU
ACCEPT A PERSON WITH ALL
IT'S FAILURES, HUMILITY, UGLY
POINTS AND NONETHELESS,
THE PERSON IS ABSOLUTE FOR YOU
EVERYTHING THAT MAKES LIFE
WORTH LIVING. YOU SEE PER-
FECTION IN IMPERFECTION ITSELF.
AND THAT'S HOW WE SHOULD
LEARN TO LOVE THE WORLD."

SLAVOJ ŽIŽEK

Play no. 7

Craig Taylor

Play no. 48

Play no. 7

(A woman stands near the revolving door of an office block in Holborn, London, sandwich in hand. She speaks into a mobile phone)

Yeah.
Yeah.
Yeah.
Yeah.
Yeah. Oh yeah.
(pause)
(laughing) Yes.
Yeah.
Yeah.
Yeah.
Yeah.
Yeah.
Yeah.
Yeah.
(pause)
(affronted) Yes.
(confirming) Yes.
Yes, yes, yes.
Aw. Yeah.
Yes.
Yes.

(pause)
Yeah.
Oh yeah?
Yeah.
Yeah.
(pause)
(concerned) Yes.
(concerned) Yeah.
(concerned) Yeah.
(concerned) Yeah.
(sympathetic) Yeah.
(sympathetic) Yeah.
(pause)
(resolute) Yes.
Yes.
Yeah.
Yeah.
Yeah.
(with finality) Yes.
(pause)
(sceptical) Mmmm, yeah.
Yeah.
Yeah.
Yeah.
Yeah.
Yes.
Just, um, trying to eat my lunch.
I know it is.
No, I wasn't chewing into the phone.
Yes.
Yes.
Yeah.
Yeah.

We only get half an hour.
Yeah.
Yeah.
Yeah.
Yeah.
Yeah.
Yeah.
OK, Mum.
Yeah.
Yeah.
Yeah.
Yeah.
Yeah, yeah, yeah.
Bye.
Yeah.
Yeah.
Bye.
OK.
Yeah.
Yeah.
Yes.
Bye. Bye.

Play no. 48

(Two people sit at the back of a night bus making its way towards Finsbury Park, London. It is two in the morning. He has a French accent. Hers is American. His arm is around her shoulders)

Ashley: So it wasn't a real stroke. Or it wasn't a crippling stroke. Do you know what a stroke is?

Marcel: Yes.
A: I don't know how to say it in French.
M: Yes.
A: Un mal de...
M: Yes, I know what it is.
A: Well, it wasn't a major one but it was still, you know...
M: It was a stroke.
A: And when my dad phoned I could just tell it was trouble. First of all, they never call me past ten at night. They're both very aware when it comes to different timezones, with me being so far ahead.
M: French is even further.
A: France is what?
M: In my country we are later. We are one hour forward.
A: Well, England is, like, five hours later than Baltimore, so I know something was up. You get that feeling in your throat. And you know when your father comes on the phone—I don't know if this has ever happened to you—but your father comes on the phone and he sounds like some-one else?
M: You look beautiful.
A: And...
M: In this light.
A: ...and your dad. Sorry?
M: I was worried that when we got outside the club you wouldn't be as beautiful as you were inside. Not so. This bus does not have good light, but you are still beautiful.
A: Thanks.
M: Your hair.
A: That's sweet. That's really. So... but... so my dad. Sorry to go back to this.
M: No, no, no.
A: My dad told me that Mom had been making strange

noises in the night, moving the sheets, that kind of thing. When he woke up she was having a stroke. Or she had just had it.

M: We are three stops from my house right now.

A: And. And so he got her to the hospital as fast as he could, which was lucky because our car? It's a wonder anyone can even drive the thing with its back end almost ninety percent rusted off. My dad walks everywhere now because we've only been at this new house for six months. He's all about walking. It used to be biking but then he was like 'No, you can only begin to understand a city if you walk its streets.' That kind of thing. So it was just lucky that when he turned the ignition the car actually started. He drove there as fast as he could.

M: Is she dead?

A: No it was just a small stroke. A petit...

M: This was your mother who had the stroke?

A: Yes.

M: And your father is black?

A: Yes.

M: And your mother is white?

A: Yes. And, you know, her recovery has just been amazing. She did the whole walking on a treadmill, the whole physical therapy thing. Her face after it happened was twisted. It was like the nerve endings had been damaged. But somehow she's really improved it through the exercises and she looks, I'd say, about ninety-five percent as good as she looked before. If you knew her before you might be able to tell, but it's not like people stare.

M: Why do they stare?

A: No, they don't stare. She's recovered.

M: And are your parents able to hold hands in public?

A: Oh they're totally affectionate. I've been so proud of my

dad, how he's handled it? Out of all my friends' parents I'd say eighty percent are divorced. So my parents are in the minority. But they're so in love, so there for each other, kissing at the table, that kind of stuff, which is kind of weird when it's people that age. But you know what's really weird? The only lasting effect of the stroke is that my mom will just forget easy words for things around her. Like the water will be running in the sink? And she'll say, 'Turn off the...' And she'll point at it and sort of shake her fingers it, and I'll be like, 'Mom, do you mean the faucet?' And she'll say, 'Yes, the faucet.' That kind of stuff happens all the time, and I know it's got something to do with the stroke.
M: I love your black skin.
A: And... sorry?
M: I love the way it gets darker around your wrinkles. Around your eyes you are very black.
A: Thanks.
M: We are two more stops from my house now. It is up this hill. That's the park over there I told you about. And that is the store where I do my shopping. It's owned by Arabs. (pause)
A: So, I mean, not to keep dwelling on this. I guess what I meant to say is that my mother is OK. But it just makes you think how precious life is. And how...
M: You've heard of The Strokes, right?
A: The what?
M: A band. They are called The Strokes. Just because you were mentioning strokes one second ago.
A: I guess I've heard of them.
M: They are very popular.
A: I don't even, you know, have a stereo over here.
M: I have a Sony stereo. The new Strokes CD is very good. You will like them. I am going to play two of their songs for

you when we get to my place. Number five is very fast. Number one is slower. I think number five is better but it will be interesting to hear what you say. Is that fine? (pause) Do you think that's fine?
A: Sure.
M: Do you like rock and roll?
A: Yeah, I sort of like everything.
M: Or do you like rap music all the time?

YOU ARE THE

LAST

GENERATION

THAT WILL

DIE

EVERYONE ON EARTH IS FEELING THE SAME WAY THAT YOU DO

Modern Love

Andrew McLuhan

Dear Five,

The reception's fine, but we're breaking up.

I regret that it's come to this, that I've been forced to resort to ink and paper.

I'm exhausted. I've shared so much with you; I've taken you everywhere, made sure you're charged and up to date. I've kept you safe and dry. We've slept together, awoke together.

I've loved the way you feel in my hands—your screen under my thumbs, the way you make me look in photos, that warm spot in my pocket.

A new version came out recently, the Six, and I'm sorry to say that I wanted it—I wanted it so bad. But I felt disloyal to you, Five. After all we shared together.

It felt disloyal. It felt wrong.

And what's up with that?

Really, I've given you so much and you've given me nothing back but anxiety over your safety and security. I couldn't forgive myself if I let anything happen to you—I don't know what I'd do without you.

I mean, if (God forbid!) you were lost or destroyed, I could get another. And it would suck to have to set up and rebuild all my contacts and everything. But it could be done.

But what would I do without you, or any of your kind? It's only been a few years, but I can't imagine how I would function without you, either personally or professionally.

And frankly, that disturbs me.

I used to pride myself on being self-sufficient—and I'm not any longer. More than that, I'm not even sure who I am without you. I don't think that's healthy for either of us.

I don't even know why I'm writing this. I guess for myself—it's not like you care—and maybe that's the problem here.

Maybe someday they'll come up with a version that can give back some of the love. Until then, I think I need some time apart.

I'm sorry.

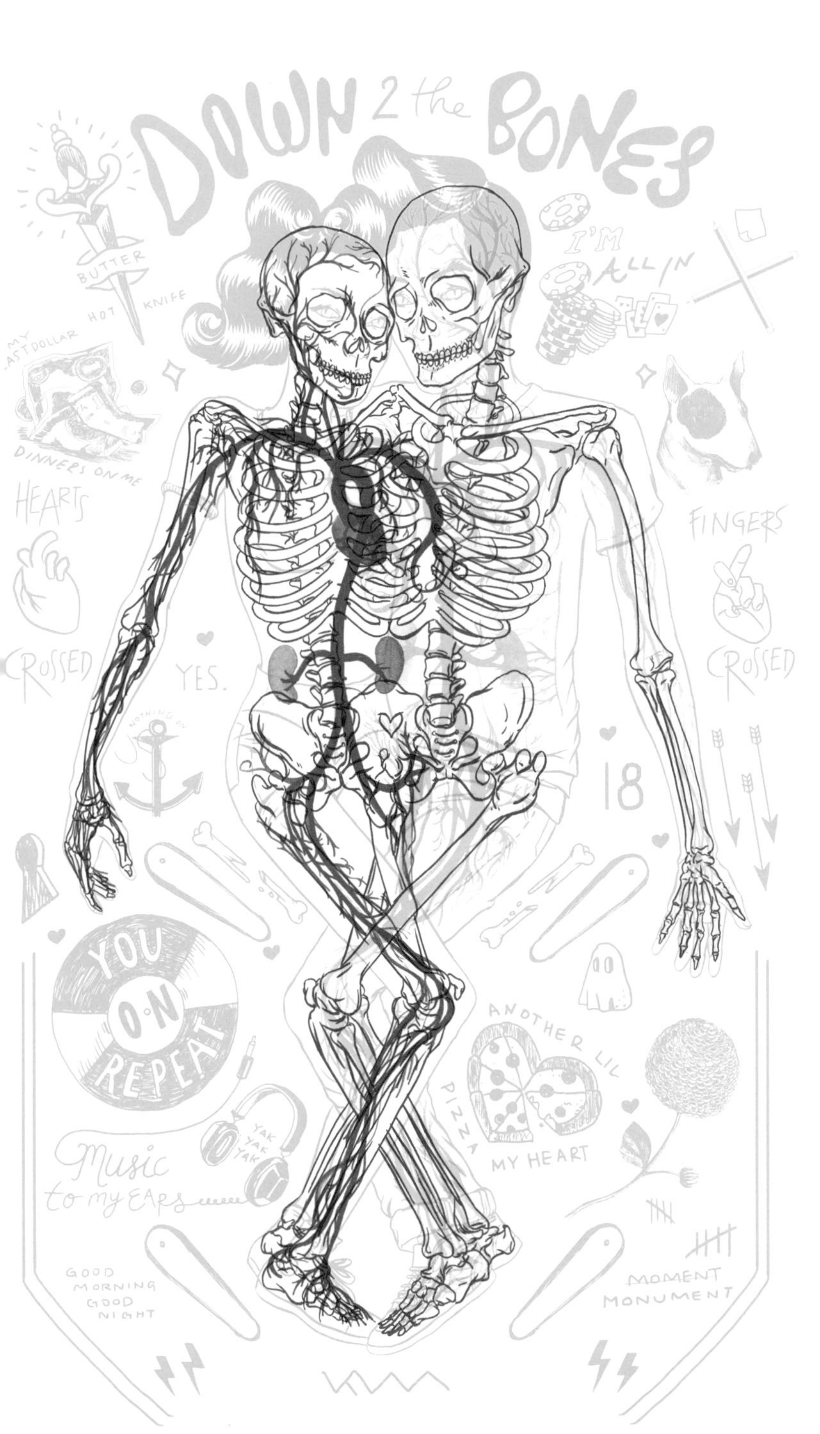
DOWN 2 the BONES
BUTTER
HOT KNIFE
MY LAST DOLLAR
DINNERS ON ME
I'M ALL IN
HEARTS
CROSSED
YES.
NOTHING ON
FINGERS
CROSSED
18
YOU ON REPEAT
ANOTHER LIL
PIZZA
MY HEART
YAK YAK YAK
Music to my EARS
GOOD MORNING GOOD NIGHT
MOMENT
MOMENT MONUMENT

no but do you ever feel bad sometimes

have you noticed that when you introduce your friends to each other they become better friends with one another than either ever was with you

have you noticed that when
people ask you for something

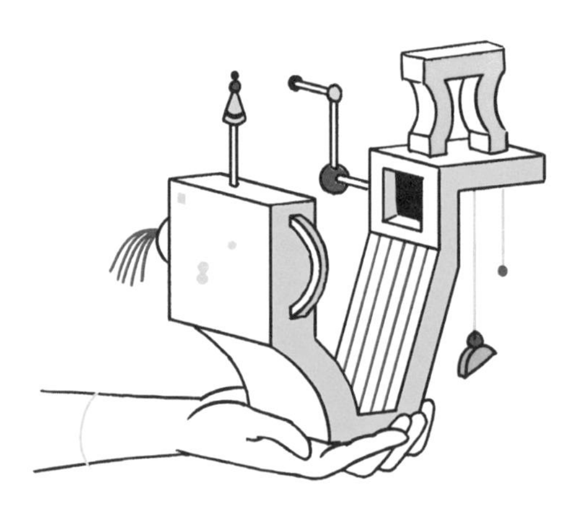

you give them a thing that is not
quite like what they asked for,
in ways that make them uncomfortable

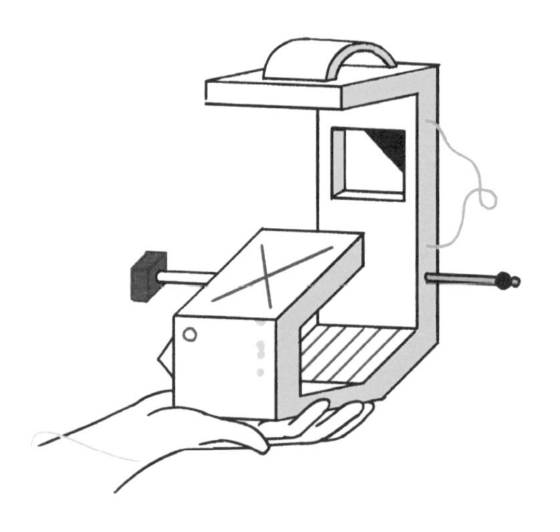

have you noticed you are often late

but never on time

bad at sports and worse at dancing

bad at the sundry QTEs of life

I don't like to do anything extemporaneously.

have you noticed that when you meet someone new their face fades as the months go by

you bore people – have you noticed that

have you noticed that loving someone
is like pouring water into a well

you don't pour water into a well
you get water out of a well

your lover is a deep dark delicious well
& you're nothing but a bucket

not even a cool bucket

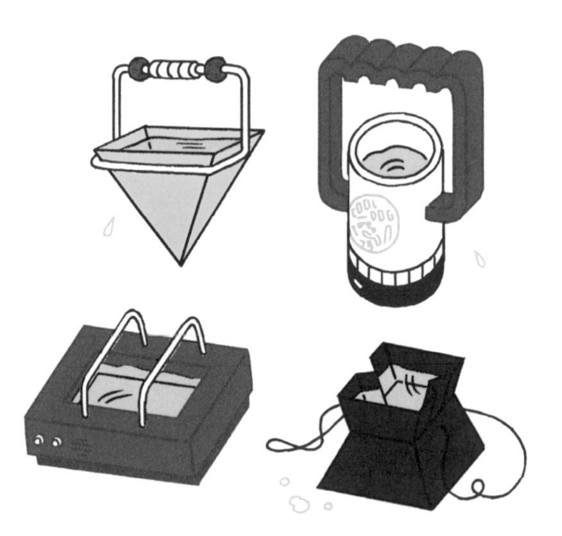

a lackluster ordinary bucket —
that feels so heavy but holds so little

hh

shhh

go to bed.

Love à la Mode

Eric McLuhan

The poet, T.S. Eliot, once observed that there were just four possible modes of conversation:

Conversation with self
Conversation with God
Conversation with an other
Conversation with others

Now, we have familiar names for each of these modes of conversation:

Conversation with God we call prayer.
Conversation with an other is dialogue, of course.
Conversation with others is discussion.
Conversation with self we call soliloquy or monologue.

This prompts the question, are there not, similarly, four modes of love? For isn't love a kind of conversation? The four modes of love, then, are as follows:

Love of God
Love of self
Love of an other
Love of others

One manifestation of God's love for us is that we exist, so love and being are at this level synonymous. Love is the ground of all being. It follows that all love however pure or imperfect has its source in God's love.

What does this analysis omit?

Is love of self necessarily a kind of narcissism, or is narcissism a perversion of self-love, a reversal? What is it, really?

Where then does sentimental love find its home? Or its relative, romantic love; and its shadow, unrequited love?

Is love of things actually love or something else?

What about love of animals, pets, which can love us in return?

Is simple affection or fondness also a kind of love? A degree of love?

And desire, covetousness? Desire is never really about the other, but about *me*.

Not love, exactly, but a mode of greed? Of lust?

And then there is the "dark side," that is, disaffection and hate. Can we not come to realizations about love by studying hate, its opposite?

Are there four modes of hate?

Each of the modes of love has a reversal, a perversal... Jealousy is not so much a form of hate as it is a form of anger.

Envy?

Pride?

The martyr: “Greater love than this hath no man, that a man lay down his life for his friends.”

I am ready
To come back
I've been here
For some time
And missed your voice
In my mind
Those cheeks

Q W E R T Y U I O P

31 likes

Plenty of Fish

Plenty of Fish

Plenty of Fish

Plenty of Fish

Briana Tabry

I'd oft been told about the sea
And its plentitude of fish
So catching one to call my own
Had been a lifelong wish.

I cast my hook a thousand times
But came up empty-handed
Was it the bait or my technique?
I couldn't understand it.

My sunny disposition
Had kept my temper steady,
Though part of me, too, did cry out,
"Where is this fish already?!"

Then one day like magic,
Or perhaps thanks to Poseidon,
I caught something any fisher
Surely would take pride in.

I knew right from the start
That this was not just any fry;
This was the one I'd waited for
And now I could see why.

A fish like this is very rare,
So different from the rest,

And that it chose to swim to me
Means certainly I'm blessed.

Past are the days when one could say
I'm just a wishful thinker;
It was worth the trips along the way
To fall hook, line and sinker.

z
z
z
z
z
J. MARTZ

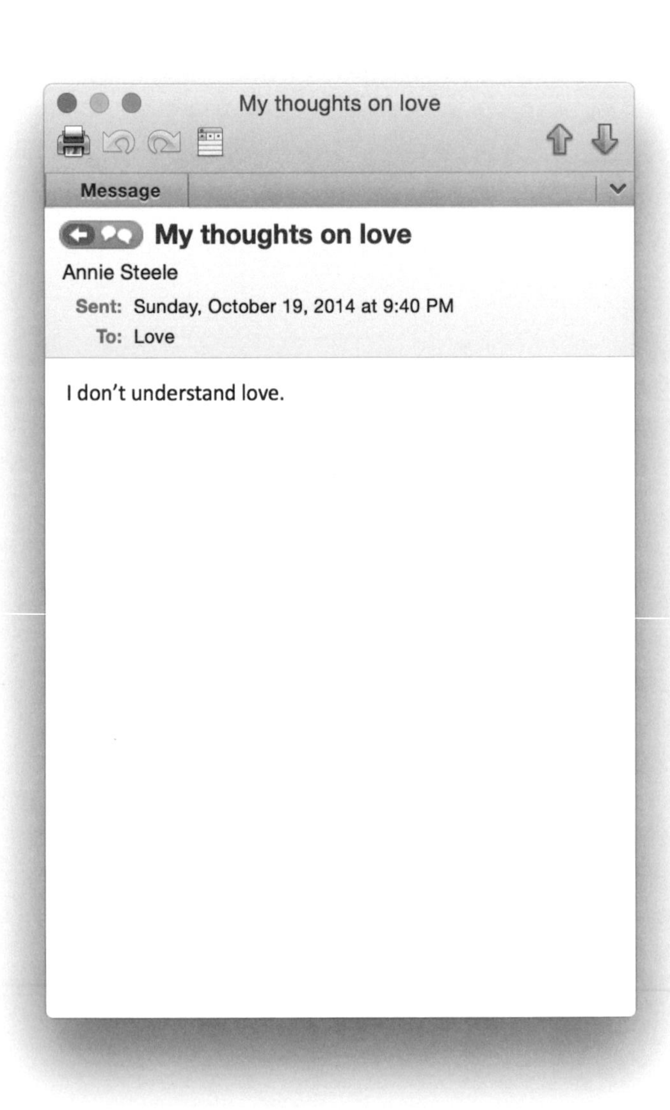
My thoughts on love
Message
My thoughts on love
Annie Steele
Sent: Sunday, October 19, 2014 at 9:40 PM
To: Love
I don't understand love.

Contributors

Tim Belonax—*timbelonax.com*
Tim Belonax is your favorite graphic designer.

Ali Burnett
Ali Burnett is on the Stickers team at Facebook. She lives in San Francisco, where she spends her time watching Back to the Future and happily eating leftovers.

Jez Burrows—*jezburrows.com*
Jez Burrows is a designer and illustrator and Englishman. He works at Facebook's Analog Research Laboratory.

Douglas Coupland—*coupland.com*
Douglas Coupland is a Canadian novelist, visual artist and designer. His first novel in 1991 was *Generation X: Tales for an Accelerated Culture*. He has published thirteen novels, a collection of short stories, seven nonfiction books, and a number of dramatic works and screenplays for film and television. Coupland's novels and visual work synthesize high and low culture, web technology, religion, and changes in human existence caused by modern technologies.

Lydia Davis
Lydia Davis is the author of one novel and four previous story collections, including *Varieties of Disturbance*, which was a finalist for the 2007 National Book Award. She is also the acclaimed translator of *Swann's Way* and *Madame*

Bovary, both of which were awarded the French American Foundation Translation Prize. She is the winner of the 2013 Man Booker International Prize.

Alain de Botton—*alaindebotton.com*
Alain de Botton was born in Zurich, Switzerland in 1969 and now lives in London. He is a writer of essayistic books that have been described as a "philosophy of everyday life." He's written on love, travel, architecture and literature. His books have been bestsellers in 30 countries.

Ray Fenwick—*rfstudio.ca*
Ray Fenwick is an illustrator, author and artist known for a playfully weird sense of humour and an obsession with type. He lives and works in Winnipeg, Manitoba, Canada. As an illustrator he has created lettering, illustration and repeat patterns for The New York Times, The Globe and Mail, Nike, O Magazine, Pentagram, Random House, Blue Q, Houghton Mifflin, Chronicle Books and many others. He has spoken about his work at universities and conferences in both Canada and the United States. As an author he created perhaps the first "typographic comic", *Hall of Best Knowledge*. The book made several "Best Graphic Novel" lists for 2008 and earned a nomination for "Best Avant-Garde Graphic Novel" from The Canadian Cartooning Awards. His most recent book, *Mascots*, was published January 2011.

Paul Ford—*postlight.com*
Paul Ford is a noted writer on technology and the web, and founder and managing partner of Postlight, a web platform and product development firm in New York City. He's currently writing a book of essays about web pages.

Sophia Foster-Dimino—*hellophia.com*
Sophia Foster-Dimino is an illustrator & cartoonist living and working in San Francisco. She graduated from the Rhode Island School of Design in 2010 with a BFA in illustration. Likes comics, videogames, biking, food, zines.

Hannah Fletcher
Hannah is a Design Program Manager at Facebook. She's powered by friendship and has claimed to have all of the feelings. Her spirit animal is a squirrel.

Melissa Gregoli
Melissa Gregoli works closely with the Product Design team at Facebook. You can usually find her at Philz Coffee drinking mint tea and talking about how napping should be a sport.

Sarah Hallacher—*sarahmak.es*
Sarah Hallacher is a designer + artist who codes living in Brooklyn, NY. Her work focuses on the social implications of technology being integrated into the most intimate parts of human life.

Erik Marinovich—*erikmarinovich.com*
Erik Marinovich is a San Francisco based lettering artist and designer, and is a co-founder of Friends of Type. Since 2009 he has drawn letters, logos and type for nice folks like: Nike, Target, Google, Hilton, Facebook, Sonos, Sharpie, The Criterion Collection, Air Canada, Gap, Ford Motor Company. Between client work, teaching, and side-projects, you'll find him at Title Case, the creative work space he co-founded that conducts workshops and lectures.

John Martz—*johnmartz.com*
Based in Toronto, Canada, John Martz is an illustrator, cartoonist, designer and the author of several books including *A Cat Named Tim and Other Stories*, *Destination X*, and the online strip *Machine Gum*. He's illustrated several books including Abbott & Costello's *Who's On First?* and Robert Heidbreder's *Black and Bitten Was Night*. John was also the founding editor of the popular illustration blog drawn.ca.

Andrew McLuhan—*umeom.com*
Andrew McLuhan is the author of *The Mutant Beavers of Delhi* (2012) and *Sasquatch of South Bay* (2015). He lives and does stuff in and around Picton, Canada.

Eric McLuhan—*ericmcluhan.com*
Eric McLuhan has over 50 years' experience teaching literature, media, culture, communication theory and high-speed reading. He has been a pilot, sailor, radio amateur, musician, and has written and co-authored many books and articles. He's spoken about communication at the Vatican on 3 occasions, at Facebook Toronto on innovation and the United Nations on the present renaissance.

Kristal Melson—*she-force-feeds.com*
Born and raised in Singapore, Kristal Melson has a background in graphic design and is currently making cool stuff at Facebook's headquarters in Asia Pacific. She leaves a trail of doodling behind in large unhealthy radioactive clumps that saw her intricate works being exhibited in galleries such as Gallery Nucleus in the US, Above Second Gallery in Hong Kong and Ikkan International and Kult Gallery in Singapore.

Sean Michaels—*byseanmichaels.com*
Sean Michaels is an internationally bestselling writer, critic and founder of the pioneering music blog Said the Gramophone. His debut novel, *Us Conductors*, reimagines the story of the theremin; it was awarded the 2014 Giller Prize. Sean lives in Montreal.

Tucker Nichols—*tuckernichols.com*
Tucker Nichols is an artist based in Northern California. His work has been featured at the Drawing Center in New York, the San Francisco Museum of Modern Art, the Denver Art Museum, Den Frie Museum in Copenhagen, and the Asian Art Museum in San Francisco. His drawings have been published in McSweeney's, The Thing Quarterly, Nieves Books and the Op-Ed pages of The New York Times.

Nous Vous—*nousvous.eu*
Nous Vous is Jay Cover, William Edmonds, and Nicolas Burrows. They collaborate on a broad range of projects including illustration & graphic design commissions, exhibitions, curatorial work, publishing and teaching. They are based in London.

Carissa Potter—*carissapotter.com*
Carissa Potter lives and works in Oakland, California. Her prints and small-scale objects reflect her hopeless romanticism through their investigations into public and private intimacy. Speaking both humorously and poignantly to the human condition, Carissa's work touches chords we all can relate to - exploring situations we've all experienced at some point in our lives and conveying messages we simply long to hear. Carissa Potter is a founding member of Colpa Press and founder of People I've Loved.

Nathaniel Russell—*nathanielrussell.com*
Nathaniel Russell was born and raised in Indiana. After college, Russell spent several years in the San Francisco Bay Area making posters, record covers, and woodcuts. He returned to his home city of Indianapolis and now spends his time creating drawings, fake fliers, bad sculptures, wood shapes, and music. Russell's work is regularly shown around the world in both traditional galleries and informal spaces, usually surrounded by an expanding list of friends, collaborators, and like-minded folk. He frequently returns to his second home of California to work with friends on projects as varied as murals, print workshops, and backyard musical performances.

Sandra Savage
Sandra found her voice amongst the support of wonderful women and fellow writers who had survived cancer, divorce, betrayal and 'life'. She's discovered, while working on her second novel what's really important in life is how you deal with it, not who you are. She's a former high-tech geek/ product director (from Adobe, Macromedia, etc.) turned executive chef and now Facebook's catering manager. Her "voice" is still about what really matters, and, in the end, if you didn't smile, laugh or giggle today, please call her. She has some great stories from Minnesota she'd love to share—and more importantly, she'd love to hear about you.

Simon Sok—*simonsok.com*
Simon grew up in Tennessee but now lives in Brooklyn, works at Facebook, and designs all sorts of graphical things. He's keen on experimental design (both digital and analog) with an emphasis on process. He enjoys collecting house plants and hopes to retire as a horticulturalist one day.

Leanne Shapton—*leanneshapton.com*
Leanne Shapton is a Canadian illustrator, author, and publisher based in New York City. She is the author of *Important Artifacts* and *Swimming Studies*, winner of the 2012 National Book Critics Circle Award for Autobiography.

Annie Steele
Annie Steele is a researcher on Facebook's Search team.

Briana Tabry
Briana is a multilingual writer who loves sushi, crossword puzzles, and making people laugh. She composed the poem in this book after dating her boyfriend Mark for exactly one month. Today they are happily married and the proud parents of Hudson, the cutest kid in the world.

Craig Taylor—*craigdtaylor.com*
Craig Taylor is the author of *Londoners: The Days and Nights of London Now*. He is the editor of Five Dials magazine.

Stéphanie Verge
Stéphanie Verge is the deputy editor of Reader's Digest (Canada). Previously, she was an associate editor at Toronto Life, during which time she won a National Magazine Award for her piece about the spread of infectious diseases in Ontario hospitals. She is the co-author of *The Bar Chef: A Modern Approach to Cocktails.*

Acknowledgments

Thanks to everybody who helped this book into existence, including—but not limited to—Andy Welfle for editing assistance, Matt Stratton for legal wrangling, Stephin Merritt for history's greatest love song, and all employees who submitted work.